YOUTH TRACK

A LEADER'S GUIDE FOR WALKING THROUGH THE BIBLE
USING STORIES ABOUT YOUTH

HAROLD F. WILLIAMS

WESTBOW
PRESS®
A DIVISION OF THOMAS NELSON
& ZONDERVAN

WestBow Press books may be ordered through booksellers or by contacting:

WestBow Press
A Division of Thomas Nelson & Zondervan
1663 Liberty Drive
Bloomington, IN 47403
www.westbowpress.com
844-714-3454

All scripture quotations are taken from the Contemporary English Version®, Copyright © 1995 American Bible Society. All rights reserved.

ISBN: 978-1-9736-9872-2 (sc)
ISBN: 978-1-9736-9871-5 (e)

Library of Congress Control Number: 2023909480

Print information available on the last page.

WestBow Press rev. date: 05/30/2023

Forward

Premise: This guide is not a "read it and talk about it" guide. Most youth are smart enough to do that themselves and will certainly know if that is how you teach a lesson. This guide only gives you a starting point. It is up to you to read, study, and research the suggested topic and to create a lesson that specifically applies to your youth and their lives.

As a class leader you should know your students, what is happening in their lives at home, school, and where they live. You are in a prime position to teach them and to learn about and discuss their spiritual and temporal growth - where they are and where they are going. For example, a class of mostly middle school students would be very different from a class of high school seniors. Focus on who they are, where they want to be and how they want to live their lives as Christian believers.

This "walk through the Bible" was inspired by members of my youth Sunday morning class. One year at the start of a new session, I asked what they would like to study in the coming year. One of the students (who rarely said much) suggested we talk about teenagers in the Bible. Members of the class agreed, and we started - somewhat randomly during that first year - to base weekly lessons on youth in the Bible. The interest shown by the students made me believe that other class leaders might want to use the same information. Following that first year several folks asked for the modified list of "youth" now included in Table 1.

Some of the stories may be familiar although the story may have almost ignored the youth involved. For example, look up the story of Rhoda in Acts 12. I've heard this story many times talking about the disciples gathering and Peter's miraculous release from prison. But do you know who Rhoda is and what an intriguing story this is from her life? How about feeding the 5,000 and the boy that had a little food. He didn't get much attention; we don't even know his name. The same things can occur with our own youth in events of their lives.

One of the most important things during each lesson was addressing what was going on in their lives and how the Bible might - and often does - relate to their daily experiences. They can relate their current culture and teen challenges to similar issues for young people for the thousands of years since these Bible stories were recorded.

No two people will use each lesson in the same manner. But get involved with the youth; find out what is going on in their world. Relate their world and their beliefs to the Biblical background, always stressing their background relationship to the Christian story - of Jesus' sacrifice and blessing to us all.

Quotations from the Bible are taken from the Contemporary English Version (CEV), Text Copyright © 1995, American Bible Society.

Contact the author of this copyrighted Leader's Guide for more information about the Guide at: publisher@youthtrack.faith

Contents

Suggestions on How to Use This Guide:

Content: Each page is formatted for one week's lesson with lots of room for your notes. At the left is a generalized historical timeline with historical dates for the stories. Each page has the Biblical reference for the full scriptural story (add or shrink as you desire).

The page also has a "suggested" key verse from that scripture to use as the focus for your lesson. Also included is a list of "suggested" key people. All of this can change based on your knowledge of your students, what is happening in their lives, and what you want to teach using the youth in the scripture as a focus. For example, the story about the prodigal son might focus on the prodigal son - but it could focus on the older brother or the loving and forgiving father.

Following the suggestions are some questions or comments about youth to focus on during your lesson. Many of these came from the youth themselves. There will be more "characteristics" introduced during your class but discussions around the challenges to the youth of today are always interesting whether they follow your lesson plan or not.

After the questions and comments is a lesson summary taken from the scripture. This section does not always include every verse in the scripture. When teaching the lesson, different students are asked to volunteer to read a single reference from a Bible, usually with pauses after each reading for discussion or explanation as needed.

The remainder of each page and the reverse side is for your notes when preparing for the class time and for your students as you desire. You must work! Cultural questions are always interesting as our youth live in a very different world than when these Bible stories were first recorded. The Internet provides a fantastic tool for research but of course you must be careful. And whenever possible relate your Old Testament stories to long-term understanding of our heavenly Father and the changes brought about through the life and crucifixion of his Son.

Lesson Sequence: Sequence of these lessons is not critical. In this Guide they are organized historically based on when they occurred (according to some sources). Individual events within your class, your hometown, or the world may lead you in other directions. You may want to focus on the birth and life of Jesus in December and Easter stories during that part of the Christian calendar. Or you may want to select certain lessons that match the theme of a summer camp or weekend retreat. Always remember who you are teaching and that you are helping them grow as strong Christian persons.

Multiple Lessons; Same Individual: Most of the stories are about a single individual and event. However, in practice I have found the stories of several youth throughout the remainder of their lives have been very instructive - individuals such as Ruth, David, Daniel, and Esther. Multiple class sessions may be needed to fully discuss the youth and their development over large parts of all the lessons. That's your decision.

<u>Youth</u>? A few of the lessons may not actually be about "youth" although many popular settings of familiar Bible stories assume that the person was a youth. For example, one reference about Isaac said that he may have been as old as the mid-30's before he and Abraham made the trip for Isaac to be sacrificed. Make your own decisions about your own research and what to use in the lessons. Some lessons may not even be applicable to what is happening in your students' world at a particular time; don't use it! The lessons should be a good opportunity to discuss the stories in relation to what your youth may need.

LESSON 1: Lot's Family

Pre-1500
1500 BC
1400 BC
1300 BC
1200 BC
1100 BC
1000 BC
900 BC
800 BC
700 BC
600 BC
500 BC
400 BC
300 BC
200 BC
100 BC
Christian Era
100 CE
200 CE
300 CE
400 CE
500 CE
600 CE
700 CE
800 CE
900 CE
1000 CE
1100 CE
1200 CE
1300 CE
1400 CE
1500 CE
1600 CE
1700 CE
1800 CE
1900 CE
2000 CE
2100 CE

Scripture: Genesis 19:12-29

Suggested Key Verse: Genesis 19:15-16 [15]Early the next morning the two angels tried to make Lot hurry and leave. They said, "Take your wife and your two daughters and get out of here as fast as you can! If you don't, every one of you will be killed when the LORD destroys the city."[16] At first, Lot just stood there. But the LORD wanted to save him. So, the angels took Lot, his wife, and his two daughters by the hand and led them out of the city.

Suggested Key People: Lot's family, angels, citizens of Sodom.

What does this story tell the youth of today? God's readiness and ability to judge and forgive our sins; lasting consequences of sin. The choices you make will affect your lives. God remembers his promises to his people. Where are your choices and promises leading? Do you ever laugh at other's (especially family, adult) suggestions? What did Lot's daughters think about the death of their mother?

Lesson Summary:

Background: Lot was Abraham's nephew but was treated much as his brother. Their families had grown large so they separated. Lot chooses to move to Sodom.

Genesis 19:12-14 Angels warn Lot to remove his family from Sodom; Lot encourages the men engaged to his daughters to leave with them; they laugh.

Genesis 19:15-17 Angels try to get Lot and family to hurry; run for it; don't look back.

Genesis 19:18-22 Lot asks the angel for a closer place of refuge; angel agrees.

Genesis 19:23-26 Sodom is destroyed – people, cities, land, trees and grass. But Lot's wife looks back and is turned into a block of salt.

Genesis 19:27-29 Abraham looks at the destruction and remembers God's promise to Lot's family.

Leader's Research and Student Notes.

_____

_____

_____

_____

_____

_____

_____

_____

_____

_____

_____

_____

_____

_____

_____

_____

_____

Beliefs, Thoughts, Drawings, Scribbles, Doodles.

LESSON 2: Young Isaac

Pre-1500
1500 BC
1400 BC
1300 BC
1200 BC
1100 BC
1000 BC
900 BC
800 BC
700 BC
600 BC
500 BC
400 BC
300 BC
200 BC
100 BC
Christian Era
100 CE
200 CE
300 CE
400 CE
500 CE
600 CE
700 CE
800 CE
900 CE
1000 CE
1100 CE
1200 CE
1300 CE
1400 CE
1500 CE
1600 CE
1700 CE
1800 CE
1900 CE
2000 CE
2100 CE

Scripture: Genesis 18-22:18

Suggested Key Verse: Genesis 22:18 [18]"You [Abraham] have obeyed me, and so you and your descendants will be a blessing to all nations on earth."

Suggested Key People: Abraham, Isaac, Sarah, Angel

What does this story tell the youth of today? Abraham's belief in God's will; Isaac's faith in his father. Would you have this much faith? How can you tell if God is speaking to you? In your life do you ever listen for God? You might get his reply from friends, family or circumstances but always be listening. God does care.

Lesson Summary:

Background: Abraham and Sarah are quite old. Abraham has three visitors who unknowingly are angels. Abraham and Sarah feed them and they promise Sarah will have a son within a year. Sarah laughs. God says nothing is too difficult for him and keeps the promise. Isaac is born and some years later God decides to test Abraham.

Genesis 22:2-5 God decides to test Abraham. He sends Abraham and Isaac to a mountain where they are to make a sacrifice to God.

Genesis 22:6-8b Abraham and Isaac reach the mountain. Abraham carries hot coals and a knife to the top of the mountain; Isaac carries the wood. Isaac asks about a lamb for the sacrifice. Abraham answers that God will provide the lamb.

Genesis 22:8c-10 They reach the place God has chosen; Abraham builds an altar. Abraham ties Isaac on the wood on the altar and gets ready to kill his son.

Genesis 22:11-14 The angel calls to Isaac not to harm his son. He knows that Abraham truly obeys God.

Genesis 22:15-19 Abraham sees a ram and sacrifices it rather than his son. The Lord's angel calls again with a promise of a large family. His descendants will be more numerous than the stars in the sky and will be a blessing to all nations on the earth.

Leader's Research and Student Notes.

_____

_____

_____

_____

_____

_____

_____

_____

_____

_____

_____

_____

_____

_____

_____

_____

Beliefs, Thoughts, Drawings, Scribbles, Doodles.

LESSON 3: Rebekah

Pre-1500
1500 BC
1400 BC
1300 BC
1200 BC
1100 BC
1000 BC
900 BC
800 BC
700 BC
600 BC
500 BC
400 BC
300 BC
200 BC
100 BC
Christian Era
100 CE
200 CE
300 CE
400 CE
500 CE
600 CE
700 CE
800 CE
900 CE
1000 CE
1100 CE
1200 CE
1300 CE
1400 CE
1500 CE
1600 CE
1700 CE
1800 CE
1900 CE
2000 CE
2100 CE

Scripture: Genesis 24

Suggested Key Verse: Genesis 24:50 [50] Laban and Bethuel answered, "The Lord has done this. We have no choice in the matter. [51] Take Rebekah with you; she can marry your master's son, just as the Lord has said." [52] Abraham's servant bowed down and thanked the Lord.

Suggested Key People: Abraham, servant, angel, Rebekah, Rebekah's family, Isaac.

What does this story tell the youth of today? Abraham's belief in God's will continues to be shown; servant's faith in Abraham and God; belief in Rebekah's parents; parent's willingness to entertain strangers; Rebekah's kindness to strangers; Rebekah's desire to go immediately. Do you have belief and faith? Do you pray about major questions or challenges? Are you willing to entertain and be kind to strangers? Would you be willing to take a major leap of faith?

Lesson Summary:

Background: Abraham is very old and very successful. He directs his most trusted servant to choose a wife for his son from among his relatives in the land where he was born. The servant is concerned that he might fail to find such a wife. Abraham tells the servant that the Lord will send his angel ahead to help him find a wife for Isaac.

Genesis 24:10-21 The servant loads his camels with gifts and sets out for the city where Abraham's brother lived. Upon his arrival Rebekah offers to give him a drink and water his camels. This was a sign to the servant that Rebekah is the choice.

Genesis 24:22-32 The servant gives Rebekah gold presents and asks about her family and a place to spend the night. Rebekah invites the servant to her parents' house and tells her family everything. The servant explains all to Rebekah's family. He says he prayed to find a wife for Isaac and to be treated fairly.

Genesis 24:33-61 The family agrees the Lord is behind the servant's search. Rebekah agrees to go with the servant almost immediately and prepares to travel.

Genesis 24:62-67 Rebekah recognizes Isaac as they approach his home. Isaac is told everything that happened and Rebekah becomes his wife.

Leader's Research and Student Notes.

_____

_____

_____

_____

_____

_____

_____

_____

_____

_____

_____

_____

_____

_____

_____

Beliefs, Thoughts, Drawings, Scribbles, Doodles.

LESSON 4: Jacob

Scripture: Genesis 25:7-11, 19-34

Suggested Key Verse: Genesis 22b-23 [22b]Finally she asked the Lord why her twins were fighting. [23]and he told her:

> "Your two sons will become
> two separate nations.
> The younger of the two (*i.e., Jacob*)
> will be stronger,
> and the older son (*i.e., Esau*)
> will be his servant."

Suggested Key People: Isaac, Rebekah, Esau, Jacob

What does this story tell the youth of today? Not really a "youth" story but completes a story about the three patriarchs of the Jewish people. God had chosen Jacob before his birth. Jacob's name later changed to "Israel", the name used for the entire nation of his descendants. Did the parents share the Lord's choice of the second son with the twins? What effect would that have as they grew up? Do you respect your immediate family? And your "family" of friends and others? Can you be careless in your decisions? Do you pray when you need guidance? Do you ask your family to help through troubling times? Do you appreciate what you have?

Lesson Summary:

Genesis 25:7-11,19-20a Abraham dies and his sons Isaac and Ishmael bury him beside his wife. When Isaac is 40 years old, he marries Rebecca.

Genesis 25:20b-23 Having no children for 20 years, Isaac asks the Lord to let Rebecca have a child. The Lord answers his prayer. Rebecca is going to have twins because she could feel them fighting before they were born. The Lord tells her about the twins becoming two nations; the younger will be stronger; the older will be his servant.

Genesis 25:24-28 Rebekah gives birth; the first baby is named Esau; the second Jacob.

Genesis 25:29-32 Much later Esau comes home hungry and Jacob asks him to sell his birthrights as the first-born for some stew that Jacob was cooking.

Genesis 25:33-34 Esau promises Jacob his birthrights for the food. After eating Esau just walks away, showing how little he thought of his rights as the first-born.

Leader's Research and Student Notes.

_____

_____

_____

_____

_____

_____

_____

_____

_____

_____

_____

_____

_____

_____

Beliefs, Thoughts, Drawings, Scribbles, Doodles.

LESSON 5: Joseph

Pre-1500
1500 BC
1400 BC
1300 BC
1200 BC
1100 BC
1000 BC
900 BC
800 BC
700 BC
600 BC
500 BC
400 BC
300 BC
200 BC
100 BC
Christian Era
100 CE
200 CE
300 CE
400 CE
500 CE
600 CE
700 CE
800 CE
900 CE
1000 CE
1100 CE
1200 CE
1300 CE
1400 CE
1500 CE
1600 CE
1700 CE
1800 CE
1900 CE
2000 CE
2100 CE

Scripture: Genesis 37:2b-34

Suggested Key Verse: [17b] Joseph left and found his brothers in Dothan. [18] But before he got there, they saw him coming and made plans to kill him. [19] They said to one another, "Look, here comes the hero of those dreams! [20] Let's kill him and throw him into a pit and say that some wild animal ate him. Then we'll see what happens to those dreams."

Suggested Key People: Jacob, Joseph, Reuben, the brothers.

What does this story tell the youth of today? A father's love is special; playing "favorites" is not. Jealousy can have bad results. In this story the seemingly "bad" results ended up as the results for God's plan. Is it hard to be the oldest child? Youngest child? No brothers or sisters? Are you often jealous of family or friends? Do you think God has a plan for your life?

Lesson Summary:

Genesis 37:2b-4 Joseph is 17, always telling his father, Jacob, bad things about his brothers. His father loves Joseph more than his other sons and gave him a special coat.

Genesis 37:5-11 Joseph told his brothers what he dreamed—that he would be king over them. Joseph told his father that all the family would all bow down to him.

Genesis 37:12-17a Jacob sends Joseph to look for his brothers who are tending sheep.

Genesis 37:117b-24 The brothers see Joseph coming and plan to kill him. But the older brother, Reuben, wants to throw him in a well and later return him to his father. The brothers pull off his special coat and throw Joseph in a well.

Genesis 37:25-34 A caravan from Gilead comes by and Joseph is sold to them. The special coat is dipped in goat's blood and the brothers tell Jacob that he was torn to pieces by a wild animal. Jacob recognized the coat and mourned for Joseph.

Leader's Research and Student Notes.

_____

_____

_____

_____

_____

_____

_____

_____

_____

_____

_____

_____

_____

_____

_____

_____

_____

_____

Beliefs, Thoughts, Drawings, Scribbles, Doodles.

LESSON 6: Miriam

Pre-1500
1500 BC
1400 BC
1300 BC
1200 BC
1100 BC
1000 BC
900 BC
800 BC
700 BC
600 BC
500 BC
400 BC
300 BC
200 BC
100 BC
Christian Era
100 CE
200 CE
300 CE
400 CE
500 CE
600 CE
700 CE
800 CE
900 CE
1000 CE
1100 CE
1200 CE
1300 CE
1400 CE
1500 CE
1600 CE
1700 CE
1800 CE
1900 CE
2000 CE
2100 CE

Scripture: Exodus 2:1-10

Suggested Key Verse: Exodus 2:7 [7]At once the baby's older sister came up and asked, "Do you want me to get a Hebrew woman to take care of the baby for you?"

Suggested Key People: A baby, the baby's older Sister (unnamed though generally believed to be Miriam), the baby's mother, the king's daughter.

What does this story tell the youth of today? This story begins as the Hebrews are slaves. All the Hebrew babies are being killed at birth. Those who do not obey are in serious trouble. How did Miriam and her mother act when the baby was born? Where did they get their strength? Where do you get your strength? Could you step in when necessary to your faith? Is God your strength and leader in your life? Could you change the course of history as Miriam did?

Lesson Summary:

Exodus 2:1-3 A Hebrew baby boy is born and hidden inside for three months. Then her mother makes a basket of reeds and hides him in the tall grass by the Nile River.

Exodus 2:4-6 Miriam watches to see what would happen. One of the king's daughters sees the basket. A servant pulls the basket out of the grass. The daughter opens the basket and feels sorry for a Hebrew baby.

Exodus 2:7-8a Immediately Miriam comes up and asks if the king's daughter needs help. She says "yes."

Exodus 2:8b-9 Miriam brings her mother. The king's daughter tells her to take care of the baby and she will be paid. The mother takes her baby home and cares for him.

Exodus 2:10 When he is old enough the mother takes him to the king's daughter to be adopted. The king's daughter names him Moses.

Leader's Research and Notes.

_____

_____

_____

_____

_____

_____

_____

_____

_____

_____

_____

_____

_____

_____

_____

_____

_____

_____

Beliefs, Thoughts, Drawings, Scribbles, Doodles.

LESSON 7: Bezalel

Pre-1500
1500 BC
1400 BC
1300 BC
1200 BC
1100 BC
1000 BC
900 BC
800 BC
700 BC
600 BC
500 BC
400 BC
300 BC
200 BC
100 BC
Christian Era
100 CE
200 CE
300 CE
400 CE
500 CE
600 CE
700 CE
800 CE
900 CE
1000 CE
1100 CE
1200 CE
1300 CE
1400 CE
1500 CE
1600 CE
1700 CE
1800 CE
1900 CE
2000 CE
2100 CE

Scripture: Exodus 31:1-11

Suggested Key Verse: Exodus 31:1-2 [1] The LORD said to Moses: [2] I have chosen Bezalel from the Judah tribe to make the sacred tent and its furnishings.

Suggested Key People: The Lord, Moses, Bezalel

What does this story tell the youth of today? Bezalel was 13 years old; could you or friends be called by God at that age? Bezalel was given exceptional skills; are you given special skills; do you use your gifts and skills wisely; are you trustworthy? Bezalel means "in the shadow (protection) of God" - faith in God and himself and leader Moses. Do you have that faith? Do you recognize and talk with God as Moses did?

Lesson Summary:

Exodus 31:1-2 The Lord tells Moses he has selected Bezalel to make the sacred tent.

Exodus 31:3-5 The Lord tells Moses he has filled Bezalel with his Spirit and given him the wisdom and skills to make the furnishings.

Exodus 31:6 The Lord also tells Moses that he has appointed Oholiab to work with Bezalel.

Exodus 31:7-11 The Lord describes in more detail some of the items to be created.

Leader's Research and Student Notes.

_____

_____

_____

_____

_____

_____

_____

_____

_____

_____

_____

_____

_____

_____

_____

_____

_____

_____

_____

_____

_____

_____

_____

_____

Beliefs, Thoughts, Drawings, Scribbles, Doodles.

LESSON 8: Servants to the Lord

Pre-1500
1500 BC
1400 BC
1300 BC
1200 BC
1100 BC
1000 BC
900 BC
800 BC
700 BC
600 BC
500 BC
400 BC
300 BC
200 BC
100 BC
Christian Era
100 CE
200 CE
300 CE
400 CE
500 CE
600 CE
700 CE
800 CE
900 CE
1000 CE
1100 CE
1200 CE
1300 CE
1400 CE
1500 CE
1600 CE
1700 CE
1800 CE
1900 CE
2000 CE
2100 CE

Scripture: Leviticus 27:1-7

Suggested Key Verse: Leviticus 27:1-3a [1]The Lord told Moses [2]to say to the community of Israel: If you ever want to free someone who has been promised to me, [3a] you may do so by paying the following amounts...

Suggested Key People: The Lord, Moses, Israelite nation

What does this story tell the youth of today? Understand and explain what "free someone who has been promised to me" means. Then use this story as an interlude in stories of named people to talk about culture then and now. It is very important for youth to understand the huge cultural differences between then and now, hence the timeline down the left margin of all lessons. If nothing else, talk about how a youth in 1400BC might spend the day, how they might communicate, how they interacted with friends and family, their beliefs in God. Those are all still important issues for our young people.

Lesson Summary:

Leviticus 27:1-3a The Lord tells Moses to say to the people in Israel how to free someone promised to the Lord by paying some specified amounts.

Leviticus 27:3b-7 The payment amounts vary significantly by age and gender.

Leader's Research and Student Notes.

_____

_____

_____

_____

_____

_____

_____

_____

_____

_____

_____

_____

_____

_____

_____

_____

_____

_____

_____

_____

_____

_____

_____

_____

_____

Beliefs, Thoughts, Drawings, Scribbles, Doodles.

LESSON 9: Zelophehad's Daughters

Pre-1500
1500 BC
1400 BC
1300 BC
1200 BC
1100 BC
1000 BC
900 BC
800 BC
700 BC
600 BC
500 BC
400 BC
300 BC
200 BC
100 BC
Christian Era
100 CE
200 CE
300 CE
400 CE
500 CE
600 CE
700 CE
800 CE
900 CE
1000 CE
1100 CE
1200 CE
1300 CE
1400 CE
1500 CE
1600 CE
1700 CE
1800 CE
1900 CE
2000 CE
2100 CE

Scripture: Numbers 36:1-12.

Suggested Key Verse: [10] Mahlah, Tirzah, Hoglah, Milcah, and Noah the daughters of Zelophehad obeyed the Lord and married their uncles' sons.

Suggested Key People: Daughters of Zelophehad, family leaders from the Gilead clan, Moses, God.

What does this story tell the youth of today? God of the Old Testament was a God of rules and judgement - and speaking directly to individuals. Is that still true? Does God still speak to and judge us individually? In the New Testament Jesus came to offer us salvation and forgiveness by believing His promises. The rules in the Old Testament changed over time and with the birth of our Savior, Jesus. Did Jesus say "don't follow the rules" or "understand the rules?"

Lesson Summary:

Numbers 36:1-4 Family leaders of the Gilead clan ask Moses about the distribution of land to the daughters of Zelophehad.

Numbers 36:5-6 Moses responds with the commands from God.

Numbers 36:7-9 Moses continues to explain the commands from God.

Numbers 36:10-11 The daughters of Zelophehad obey the Lord and marry as the law required.

Leader's Research and Student Notes.

_____

_____

_____

_____

_____

_____

_____

_____

_____

_____

_____

_____

_____

_____

_____

_____

_____

_____

_____

_____

_____

_____

_____

_____

_____

Beliefs, Thoughts, Drawings, Scribbles, Doodles.

LESSON 10: The Sin of Achan

Pre-1500
1500 BC
1400 BC
1300 BC
1200 BC
1100 BC
1000 BC
900 BC
800 BC
700 BC
600 BC
500 BC
400 BC
300 BC
200 BC
100 BC
Christian Era
100 CE
200 CE
300 CE
400 CE
500 CE
600 CE
700 CE
800 CE
900 CE
1000 CE
1100 CE
1200 CE
1300 CE
1400 CE
1500 CE
1600 CE
1700 CE
1800 CE
1900 CE
2000 CE
2100 CE

Scripture: Joshua 7

Suggested Key Verse: Joshua 7:1 [1]The Lord had said that everything in Jericho belonged to him. But Achan from the Judah tribe took some of the things from Jericho for himself. And so the Lord was angry with the Israelites, because one of them had disobeyed him.

Suggested Key People: The Lord, Achan, Joshua, Israelite nation.

What does this story tell the youth of today? This is another story that shows the difference in God's judgement after Jesus' crucifixion and resurrection. It also tells a lot about the culture of the chosen people, the Israelites, in the Old Testament. Today family members are no longer held accountable for the acts of the family members unless also involved. If you were a family member as a youth, how would you have felt? Do your friends make up a part of your "family?" Are you ever guilty by association? Does that hurt when unjustified? Does it hurt when justified? Does it affect your future actions? Do you ever ask God "Why?"

Lesson Summary:

Joshua 7:1 The Lord says that everything captured in Jericho belongs to him. But Achan takes some things for himself.

Joshua 7:2-5 Israel sends an army to capture another small town, Ai, but is defeated.

Joshua 7:6-9a Joshua and the leaders of Israel are sorrowful and ask the Lord "Why?"

Joshua 7:9b-15 The Lord repeats the "rules" in verse 1. He tells the people of Israel to gather everyone near the place of worship and he would show who stole from Jericho.

Joshua 7:16-22a Joshua and the Israelites gather as instructed by the Lord. He reviews the entire tribes of Israel. He identifies Achan as the guilty one.

Joshua 7:22b-26 Joshua is told to go to Achan's tent and search for the stolen property. Upon finding the property, the people of Israel stone to death Achan and his family and burn all their possessions. Then the Lord is no longer angry.

Leader's Research and Student Notes.

_____

_____

_____

_____

_____

_____

_____

_____

_____

_____

_____

_____

_____

_____

_____

Beliefs, Thoughts, Drawings, Scribbles, Doodles.

LESSON 11: Achsah

Timeline
Pre-1500
1500 BC
1400 BC
1300 BC ◄
1200 BC
1100 BC
1000 BC
900 BC
800 BC
700 BC
600 BC
500 BC
400 BC
300 BC
200 BC
100 BC
Christian Era
100 CE
200 CE
300 CE
400 CE
500 CE
600 CE
700 CE
800 CE
900 CE
1000 CE
1100 CE
1200 CE
1300 CE
1400 CE
1500 CE
1600 CE
1700 CE
1800 CE
1900 CE
2000 CE
2100 CE

Scripture: Joshua 15:13-20

Suggested Key Verse: [19] She answered, "I need your help. The land you gave me is in the Southern Desert, so I really need some spring-fed ponds for a water supply."

Suggested Key People: Joshua, Caleb, Achsah, Othniel

What does this story tell the youth of today? It finishes the stories in this series about the "promised land" that God promised Abraham. The Israelites are beginning to settle there. But there is still a long way to go as the Israelites become a nation and have many successes and failures with fulfilling their covenant with God. What happens as a people and as individuals change? What is happening with the youth in your class? Do they understand a "covenant"? With family? With others? With God?

Lesson Summary:

Joshua 15:13 Joshua distributes part of the new nation's land to Caleb.

Joshua 15:14-16 Caleb starts a war and promises his daughter, Achsah, in marriage for the capture of a major city.

Joshua 15:17 Othniel captures the city and Caleb lets him marry Achsah.

Joshua 15:18-19 Achsah tells her new husband, Othniel, to ask for a field with spring-fed ponds for a water supply. Caleb agrees.

Leader's Research and Student Notes. This story provides a good place to recap what has happened since God's covenant with Moses; where the story began, the story of the patriarchs, living in and escape from Egypt, wandering in the desert, and final entry into the promised land. Now the Israelites will begin their struggle with creating a nation.

_____

_____

_____

_____

_____

_____

_____

_____

_____

_____

_____

_____

_____

_____

_____

_____

_____

_____

_____

_____

_____

Beliefs, Thoughts, Drawings, Scribbles, Doodles.

LESSON 12: Jether and Jotham

Pre-1500
1500 BC
1400 BC
1300 BC
1200 BC
1100 BC
1000 BC
900 BC
800 BC
700 BC
600 BC
500 BC
400 BC
300 BC
200 BC
100 BC
Christian Era
100 CE
200 CE
300 CE
400 CE
500 CE
600 CE
700 CE
800 CE
900 CE
1000 CE
1100 CE
1200 CE
1300 CE
1400 CE
1500 CE
1600 CE
1700 CE
1800 CE
1900 CE
2000 CE
2100 CE

Scripture: Judges 8:13-20; 9:6-21

Suggested Key Verses: Judges 8:20 and Judges 9:21 8:20 Gideon turned to Jether, his oldest son. "Kill them!" Gideon said. But Jether was young, and he was too afraid to even pull out his sword." ... 9:21 Jotham ran off and went to live in the town of Beer, where he could be safe from his brother Abimelech."

Suggested Key People: Gideon, Jether, Jotham, Abimelech

What does this story tell the youth of today? Gideon has a lot of sons; two of them are very different. His son by the slave is very different. Does this happen in today's world for sons and daughters? Pressure can come from parents/peers. Some decisions are hard; some decisions are unpopular. Being in the majority doesn't make it right. God is in charge. If time allows, discuss the meaning of the fable of the trees.

Lesson Summary:

Judges 8:13-18a Gideon returns from battle and accuses town officials of making fun of him and his army. Gideon asks two kings about the men that were killed.

Judges 8:18b-20 Gideon finds out the deaths included his brothers and tells his oldest son, Jether, to kill the kings. Jether is young and too afraid to even pull out his sword."

Note 1: Years pass. Gideon has 70 sons and one son, Abimelech, by a slave girl.

Judges 9:6-7 Jotham, Gideon's son, hears that Abimelech is to be made king. He told a fable of the trees to the leaders including priests and military officers.

Note 2: A copy of the fable should be available for discussion if desired.

Judges 9:16-18 After the fable, Gideon's son Jotham reminds the leaders about their killing of all Gideon's other sons and Gideon's own death.

Judges 9:19-21 Jotham curses the leaders that they might be destroyed and then runs away, never to be heard of again.

Leader's Research and Student Notes.

_____

_____

_____

_____

_____

_____

_____

_____

_____

_____

_____

_____

_____

_____

_____

_____

_____

Beliefs, Thoughts, Drawings, Scribbles, Doodles.

LESSON 13: Jephthah's Daughter

Pre-1500
1500 BC
1400 BC
1300 BC
1200 BC
1100 BC
1000 BC
900 BC
800 BC
700 BC
600 BC
500 BC
400 BC
300 BC
200 BC
100 BC
Christian Era
100 CE
200 CE
300 CE
400 CE
500 CE
600 CE
700 CE
800 CE
900 CE
1000 CE
1100 CE
1200 CE
1300 CE
1400 CE
1500 CE
1600 CE
1700 CE
1800 CE
1900 CE
2000 CE
2100 CE

Scripture: Judges 11:29-40

Suggested Key Verse: Judges 11:36 [36]"Father," she said, "you made a sacred promise to the Lord, and he let you defeat the Ammonites. Now, you must do what you promised, even if it means I must die."

Suggested Key People: God, Jephthah, Jephthah's Daughter

What does this story tell the youth of today? Why would a father make such a promise? Could you find the courage as shown by his daughter? What do you think Jephthah's promise, "sacrifice to you (the Lord) whoever comes out to meet me first" meant? Was the daughter permanently assigned to duties in the temple and "died" to ever having a normal, married life; was she physically sacrificed? Should we bargain with God? Promises are serious to others also – family, friends, employers. They can have long term consequences. Do you lose the trust of family and friends if you do not keep your promises? Do broken promises affect family relationships? What differences do you see in the culture of the Old Testament and the New Testament after Jesus.

Lesson Summary:

Judges 11:29-32 Jephthah raises an army and promises the Lord that when he comes home from a victory, he will sacrifice whoever comes out to meet him first.

Judges 11:33-34 Jephthah is victorious and the first one to meet him is his daughter.

Judges 11:35-37 Jephthah is in great sorrow but his daughter says he must keep his sacred promise to the Lord. She asks for two months in the hills with her friends.

Judges 11:38-40 Jephthah agrees to her request. His daughter and friends wander in the hill country and then she goes back to her father. He did what he promised.

Leader's Research and Student Notes.

_____

_____

_____

_____

_____

_____

_____

_____

_____

_____

_____

_____

_____

_____

_____

_____

_____

_____

_____

_____

Beliefs, Thoughts, Drawings, Scribbles, Doodles.

LESSON 14: Samson

Pre-1500
1500 BC
1400 BC
1300 BC
1200 BC
1100 BC
1000 BC
900 BC
800 BC
700 BC
600 BC
500 BC
400 BC
300 BC
200 BC
100 BC
Christian Era
100 CE
200 CE
300 CE
400 CE
500 CE
600 CE
700 CE
800 CE
900 CE
1000 CE
1100 CE
1200 CE
1300 CE
1400 CE
1500 CE
1600 CE
1700 CE
1800 CE
1900 CE
2000 CE
2100 CE

Scripture: Judges 13:1-24

Suggested Key Verse: Judges 13:7c [7c]...Our son will belong to God for as long as he lives."

Suggested Key People: Samson, Manoah and wife, Angel, Delilah

What does this story tell the youth of today? God's promises; pressures from family and others; using and wasting our gifts; revenge (good or bad?); self-centered? Was Samson spoiled? Chosen? Used by God? Do all of these occur in today's world with you and your friends? What do you think of the restrictions put on Samson's life? Do you have fair or unfair restrictions? How does current culture compare to Samson's time?

Lesson Summary:

Judges 13:1 The Israelites are again disobeying the Lord so he let the Philistines take control of Israel for 40 years.

Judges 13:2-5 Manoah's wife cannot have children. An angel appears to Manoah's wife with a promise of a future son – but with specific instructions.

Judges 13:6-7 Manoah's wife tells her husband about the visitor, the son to be born, and that the son will belong to God for as long as he lives.

Judges 13:8-11 The angel returns to talk with Manoah and his wife about how the son is to be raised.

Judges 13:12-24 Manoah and his wife acknowledge that the visitor is one of the Lord's angels, and the angel visits with them. Samson is born.

Leader's Research and Student Notes. Special Notes: Samson's story is a long one and might cover several lessons if you choose - from his birth, his wives, stories of his activities, and destruction of the Philistines with God's help.

Special Notes: There are many stories about Samson in Judges 14-16. These are certain to get your students attention:

Judges 14:1-20 Samson sees a Philistine woman he wants to marry, tells his parents to "get her" for him; kills a lion with his bare hands on his way to a wedding party, and makes a "party" bet the Philistines cannot figure out a riddle.

Judges 15:1-8 Samson catches 300 foxes, ties them together in pairs, and sets them on fire to destroy the Philistine wheat fields.

Judges 16:1-22 Samson's wife, Delilah, tries to trick Samson so that he will lose his strength. Samson finally tells her the secret and Samson is captured and his eyes are poked out.

Judges 16:23-30 Samson gets revenge, prays to God for strength, and kills more Philistines when he died than he had killed during his entire life.

_____

_____

_____

_____

_____

_____

_____

_____

_____

_____

_____

_____

_____

Beliefs, Thoughts, Drawings, Scribbles, Doodles.

LESSON 15: Ruth

Pre-1500
1500 BC
1400 BC
1300 BC
1200 BC
1100 BC
1000 BC
900 BC
800 BC
700 BC
600 BC
500 BC
400 BC
300 BC
200 BC
100 BC
Christian Era
100 CE
200 CE
300 CE
400 CE
500 CE
600 CE
700 CE
800 CE
900 CE
1000 CE
1100 CE
1200 CE
1300 CE
1400 CE
1500 CE
1600 CE
1700 CE
1800 CE
1900 CE
2000 CE
2100 CE

Scripture: Ruth 1

Suggested Key Verse: Ruth 1:16b [16b]"I will go where you go, I will live where you live; your people will be my people, your God will be my God."

Suggested Key People: Ruth, Naomi

What does this story tell the youth of today? Note that one of Ruth's great grandchildren was King David. Be faithful; honor commitments; tomorrow is unknown so do your best. Are you changed by those around you; do you change those around you? Was Ruth chosen by God; is God involved in your life?

Lesson Summary:

Ruth 1:1-5 Crops in Israel fail and Naomi and family move to Moab; Naomi's husband dies; Naomi's sons marry Moab women; Naomi's sons die.

Ruth 1:6-10 The crops in Israel are better and Naomi wants to return home. Naomi tells her daughters-in-law that they had been good to her but they could stay with their own people.

Ruth 1:11-17 Ruth wants to go with her and promises that "your God will be my God."

Ruth 1:18-22 Ruth and Naomi arrive in Bethlehem

Leader's Research and Student Notes. Special Notes: Ruth's story in Ruth 2-4 is a story of blessings that can come from good choices. Those chapters can be an extension of this lesson or another lesson.

_____

_____

_____

_____

_____

_____

_____

_____

_____

_____

_____

_____

_____

_____

_____

_____

_____

_____

_____

_____

_____

_____

_____

Beliefs, Thoughts, Drawings, Scribbles, Doodles.

LESSON 16: Samuel

Pre-1500
1500 BC
1400 BC
1300 BC
1200 BC
1100 BC
1000 BC
900 BC
800 BC
700 BC
600 BC
500 BC
400 BC
300 BC
200 BC
100 BC
Christian Era
100 CE
200 CE
300 CE
400 CE
500 CE
600 CE
700 CE
800 CE
900 CE
1000 CE
1100 CE
1200 CE
1300 CE
1400 CE
1500 CE
1600 CE
1700 CE
1800 CE
1900 CE
2000 CE
2100 CE

Scripture: 1 Samuel 1:6-22, 2:11, 3:1-10

Suggested Key Verse: Samuel 3:10b [10b] "I'm listening," Samuel answered. "What do you want me to do?"

Suggested Key People: Hannah and Elkanah (parents), Samuel, Eli

What does this story tell the youth of today? God talked to Samuel's mother and father before he was born. When Samuel was young, he lived with the priest – for the rest of his life! How would that affect someone young? God guided Samuel throughout Samuel's life. Can he do the same for you? Does he? Samuel obeyed his parents and his mentor, Eli. Should you? What do you say/how do you act when you have to call a valued mentor or even a parent to task?

Lesson Summary:

Samuel 1:6-17 Hannah is distressed because she cannot have children. Eli the priest thinks she is drunk and tells her to "Sober up!" Hannah explains and Eli tells her that her prayers will be answered.

Samuel 1:19-22, 2:11 Hannah and Elkanah are blessed with a son, Samuel. When Samuel is old enough, they give him to the Lord at Shiloh for the rest of his life.

Samuel 3:1-4 Samuel serves the Lord by helping Eli the priest. One night Samuel thinks that Eli is calling him.

Samuel 3:5-8 Samuel runs to answer but Eli tells him that he did not call. This happens several times and Eli finally realizes that the Lord is calling Samuel.

Samuel 3:9-10 Eli tells Samuel to lie down and if someone calls again to answer the Lord with a question, "What do you want me to do?"

Leader's Research and Notes.

_____

_____

_____

_____

_____

_____

_____

_____

_____

_____

_____

_____

_____

_____

_____

_____

_____

_____

_____

_____

_____

_____

Beliefs, Thoughts, Drawings, Scribbles, Doodles.

LESSON 17: David

Pre-1500
1500 BC
1400 BC
1300 BC
1200 BC
1100 BC
1000 BC
900 BC
800 BC
700 BC
600 BC
500 BC
400 BC
300 BC
200 BC
100 BC
Christian Era
100 CE
200 CE
300 CE
400 CE
500 CE
600 CE
700 CE
800 CE
900 CE
1000 CE
1100 CE
1200 CE
1300 CE
1400 CE
1500 CE
1600 CE
1700 CE
1800 CE
1900 CE
2000 CE
2100 CE

Scripture: 1 Samuel 16:1-13

Suggested Key Verse: 1 Samuel 16:13b ¹³ᵇ At that moment, the Spirit of the Lord took control of David and stayed with him from then on.

Suggested Key People: The Lord, Samuel, Jesse, David, Jesse's other sons.

What does this story tell the youth of today? Was this a heavy load for David as a youth? Was it a heavy load for the brothers? It was a blessing to David as an adult. Was David remembering this when he fought Goliath? What did David and all the older brothers think of Samuel's actions? Did they understand? Does God look into our hearts today and decide where we are going or where to lead us?

Lesson Summary:

1 Samuel 16:1-3 The Lord tells Samuel that he refuses to let Saul be king any longer. He sends Samuel to visit a man named Jesse to choose one of his sons as king.

1 Samuel 16:4-5 Samuel did what the Lord told him and went to Bethlehem to see Jesse and his sons.

1 Samuel 16:6-11a Samuel notices Jesse's oldest son and assumes he is chosen to be king. But the Lord has other plans. None of Jesse's seven sons who are present are chosen. Samuel asks if there are others.

1 Samuel 16:11b-13a Jesse sends for David and the Lord immediately says that David is the one. Samuel anoints David with olive oil to be the next king.

1 Samuel 16:13b The Spirit of the Lord immediately takes control of David and stays with him from then on.

Leader's Research and Student Notes.

_____

_____

_____

_____

_____

_____

_____

_____

_____

_____

_____

_____

_____

_____

_____

_____

_____

_____

_____

_____

_____

Beliefs, Thoughts, Drawings, Scribbles, Doodles.

LESSON 18: Temple Musicians

Timeline
Pre-1500
1500 BC
1400 BC
1300 BC
1200 BC
1100 BC
1000 BC
900 BC
800 BC
700 BC
600 BC
500 BC
400 BC
300 BC
200 BC
100 BC
Christian Era
100 CE
200 CE
300 CE
400 CE
500 CE
600 CE
700 CE
800 CE
900 CE
1000 CE
1100 CE
1200 CE
1300 CE
1400 CE
1500 CE
1600 CE
1700 CE
1800 CE
1900 CE
2000 CE
2100 CE

Scripture: 1 Chronicles 25:1-8

Suggested Key Verse: [8] David assigned them their duties by asking the LORD what he wanted. Everyone was responsible for something, whether young or old, teacher or student.

Suggested Key People: The Lord, David, and Temple officials.

What does this story tell the youth of today? At the time of this story, music in the temple was limited to males. That was a part of their culture. The temple music was important to praise the Lord. Can things in today's culture limit what you can do with your life? Can individuals change or override culture? Could you? Do your best with your life; honor your responsibilities; always ask God to give you guidance in your lives.

Lesson Summary:

1 Chronicles 25:1 David and temple officials choose individuals and their descendants to be in charge of music in the temple.

1 Chronicles 25:2-6 Three men and their sons are selected to play music as ordered by the king.

1 Chronicles 25:7 There are 288 men, all skilled musicians, selected.

1 Chronicles 25:8 Each one of these men were responsible for something, whether young or old, teacher or student.

Leader's Research and Student Notes.

_____

_____

_____

_____

_____

_____

_____

_____

_____

_____

_____

_____

_____

_____

_____

_____

_____

_____

_____

_____

_____

_____

_____

Beliefs, Thoughts, Drawings, Scribbles, Doodles.

LESSON 19: Solomon

Pre-1500
1500 BC
1400 BC
1300 BC
1200 BC
1100 BC
1000 BC
900 BC
800 BC
700 BC
600 BC
500 BC
400 BC
300 BC
200 BC
100 BC
Christian Era
100 CE
200 CE
300 CE
400 CE
500 CE
600 CE
700 CE
800 CE
900 CE
1000 CE
1100 CE
1200 CE
1300 CE
1400 CE
1500 CE
1600 CE
1700 CE
1800 CE
1900 CE
2000 CE
2100 CE

Scripture: 2 Samuel 12:13-25

Suggested Key Verse: 2 Samuel 12:19b-20 [19b]"Did my son die?" he (David) asked his servants. "Yes, he did," they answered. [20]David got up off the floor; he took a bath, combed his hair, and dressed. He went into the Lord's tent and worshiped, then he went back home. David asked for something to eat, and when his servants brought him some food, he ate it.

Suggested Key People: David, Bathsheba, Solomon, officials.

What does this story tell the youth of today? Solomon was "called" from his birth as one whom the Lord loved. Many others from the Old Testament were called. Does that still happen? Are you loved by God? Do we get second chances when we sin or disobey? Do you offer second chances to those that you love – friends, family - or even strangers? Could God have a plan for you?

Lesson Summary:

2 Samuel 12:13-14 David has just disobeyed the Lord. Nathan warns David that he has been forgiven but that his newborn son will die.

2 Samuel 12:15-17 The Lord makes David's son very sick and David goes without eating; he spends the night sleeping on the floor. His officials cannot get him to get up or eat with them.

2 Samuel 12:18 The son dies after being sick for seven days and the officials are afraid to tell David.

2 Samuel 12:19-21 David finds out the boy has died. He gets up off the floor, cleans up, and then goes to the Lord's tent and worships. His officials ask why he has done this after his son dies.

2 Samuel 12:22-23 David answers that there was still hope while his son was alive and hoped that the Lord would pity him. His son is now dead; the Lord has decided.

2 Samuel 12:24-25 David comforts his wife and later she gives birth to another son and names him Solomon. The Lord loves Solomon and sends Nathan the prophet to tell David that the Lord will call him Jedidiah, a Hebrew name meaning "Loved by the Lord."

Leader's Research and Student Notes.

_____

_____

_____

_____

_____

_____

_____

_____

_____

_____

_____

_____

_____

_____

_____

_____

_____

Beliefs, Thoughts, Drawings, Scribbles, Doodles.

LESSON 20: Abishag

| Pre-1500 |
| 1500 BC |
| 1400 BC |
| 1300 BC |
| 1200 BC |
| 1100 BC |
| 1000 BC |
| 900 BC |
| 800 BC |
| 700 BC |
| 600 BC |
| 500 BC |
| 400 BC |
| 300 BC |
| 200 BC |
| 100 BC |
| Christian Era |
| 100 CE |
| 200 CE |
| 300 CE |
| 400 CE |
| 500 CE |
| 600 CE |
| 700 CE |
| 800 CE |
| 900 CE |
| 1000 CE |
| 1100 CE |
| 1200 CE |
| 1300 CE |
| 1400 CE |
| 1500 CE |
| 1600 CE |
| 1700 CE |
| 1800 CE |
| 1900 CE |
| 2000 CE |
| 2100 CE |

Scripture: 1 Kings 1-2 (Various verses)

Suggested Key Verse: 1 Kings 1:3-4 [3-4]They looked everywhere in Israel until they found a very beautiful young woman named Abishag, who lived in the town of Shunem. They brought her to David, and she took care of him. But David did not have sex with her.

Suggested Key People: King David, Abishag, Solomon, Bathsheba, Adonijah

What does this story tell the youth of today? Abishag must have been very beautiful in characteristics as well as appearance. A young woman with her attributes was looked for everywhere in Israel to be a helper and servant for an aging King David. Her name and future after King David's death is unknown. However she did have an influence on Solomon's tenure as king following his father's death. No words in the Bible are attributed to her. As a youth, you may be very important to others in your life without knowing it; God is in control. Your choices, your words, and your actions can affect others. What do you think happened to Abishag? Was she important at other times or was she just an unknown player in this story in the Old Testament?

Lesson Summary:

1 Kings 1:1-4 King David is an old man and needs someone to take care of him. Abishag is chosen.

1 Kings 1:5-6 Adonijah, the son of David, brags that he will make himself king.

1 Kings 1:15-18 Abishag is taking care of David when Bathsheba walks in. Bathsheba asks that David remembers his promise that her son Solomon would be the next king – but that Adonijah, another of David's sons has already been made king.

1 Kings 1:28-31 David tells Bathsheba that the living Lord has kept him safe and he will keep the promise he made to Bathsheba in his name: Solomon will be the next king.

1 Kings 1:49-52 But Adonijah and friends had made Adonijah king. They are afraid of what Solomon will do when he finds out. Solomon promises that he won't hurt Adonijah if he doesn't cause trouble.

1 Kings 2:13-20a Later Adonijah asks a favor of Bathsheba - to ask Solomon to let him marry Abishag. She agrees to do so.

1 Kings 2:20b-23 When Bathsheba asks Solomon to let Adonijah marry Abishag he is very upset and swears in the name of the Lord that Adonijah will die because he asked.

Leader's Research and Student Notes. Note: In the culture of this time, having sexual relations with a former king's concubine was a way of proclaiming yourself to be the new king.

_____

_____

_____

_____

_____

_____

_____

_____

_____

_____

_____

_____

_____

_____

Beliefs, Thoughts, Drawings, Scribbles, Doodles.

LESSON 21: Abijah

Pre-1500
1500 BC
1400 BC
1300 BC
1200 BC
1100 BC
1000 BC
900 BC
800 BC
700 BC
600 BC
500 BC
400 BC
300 BC
200 BC
100 BC
Christian Era
100 CE
200 CE
300 CE
400 CE
500 CE
600 CE
700 CE
800 CE
900 CE
1000 CE
1100 CE
1200 CE
1300 CE
1400 CE
1500 CE
1600 CE
1700 CE
1800 CE
1900 CE
2000 CE
2100 CE

Scripture: 1 Kings 14:1-18

Suggested Key Verse: 1 Kings 14:12 [12] That's the Lord's message to your husband. As for you, go back home, and right after you get there, your son (Abijah) will die.

Suggested Key People: Abijah, son of Jeroboam; Jeroboam, King of Israel; Jeroboam's wife; Ahijah, the prophet.

What does this story tell the youth of today? Various references and translations call Abijah a "child," a "youth", or a "boy". The next passage immediately after the Key Verse says that everyone in Israel will mourn at Abijah's funeral because he is the only one of Jeroboam's family whom the Lord is pleased with. The culture of the Old Testament is very family oriented. In today's world are the sins of parents passed on to their children? Can you be directly affected by your family and friends? Do their sins pass on to you? Jesus came to offer a new view of God's kingdom and individual choices. Can anyone be forgiven? What is your choice?

Lesson Summary:

1 Kings 14:1 King Jeroboam's son, Abijah, gets sick.

1 Kings 14:2-5 King Jeroboam sends wife in disguise to Ahijah, the prophet, to see what will happen to his son. The Lord tells Ahijah who is in disguise.

1 Kings 14:6-11 Ahijah gives very bad news to King Jeroboam's wife about her husband, and her entire family.

1 Kings 14:12-16 Ahijah gives further bad news about the death of her son, the sins of her husband, a new king and the nation of Israel.

1 Kings 14:17-18 Abijah dies as foretold by Ahijah and everyone in Israel mourns.

Leader's Research and Student Notes.

_____

_____

_____

_____

_____

_____

_____

_____

_____

_____

_____

_____

_____

_____

_____

_____

_____

_____

_____

_____

_____

Beliefs, Thoughts, Drawings, Scribbles, Doodles.

LESSON 22: Children/Young People

Pre-1500
1500 BC
1400 BC
1300 BC
1200 BC
1100 BC
1000 BC
900 BC
800 BC
700 BC
600 BC
500 BC
400 BC
300 BC
200 BC
100 BC
Christian Era
100 CE
200 CE
300 CE
400 CE
500 CE
600 CE
700 CE
800 CE
900 CE
1000 CE
1100 CE
1200 CE
1300 CE
1400 CE
1500 CE
1600 CE
1700 CE
1800 CE
1900 CE
2000 CE
2100 CE

Scripture: Proverbs 13:1-6, 20

Suggested Key Verse: Proverbs 13:20 [20] Wise friends make you wise, but you hurt yourself by going around with fools.

Suggested Key People: Solomon as the author (highly likely).

What does this story tell the youth of today? Read each verse one at a time and discuss. Do the youth accept the proverb as written? Do they apply regardless of the individual - kids, youth, adult, senior adult - parents and siblings? Has the meaning changed in over 3,000 years? Do teachings of Jesus authenticate these proverbs for Christians (think the Beatitudes in Matthew 5 and Luke 6)? One definition of a beatitude is "supreme blessedness."

Lesson Summary:

Proverbs 13:1 Accept correction from your parents.

Proverbs 13:2 Say something kind.

Proverbs 13:3 Don't talk too much.

Proverbs 13:4 Work hard; laziness won't help.

Proverbs 13:5 Hate deceit.

Proverbs 13:6 Live right; sin will destroy you.

Proverbs 13:20 Wise friends make you wise; you are hurt by going around with fools.

Leader's Research and Student Notes.

_____

_____

_____

_____

_____

_____

_____

_____

_____

_____

_____

_____

_____

_____

_____

_____

_____

_____

_____

_____

_____

_____

Beliefs, Thoughts, Drawings, Scribbles, Doodles.

LESSON 23: Boys and the Bears

Pre-1500
1500 BC
1400 BC
1300 BC
1200 BC
1100 BC
1000 BC
900 BC
800 BC
700 BC
600 BC
500 BC
400 BC
300 BC
200 BC
100 BC
Christian Era
100 CE
200 CE
300 CE
400 CE
500 CE
600 CE
700 CE
800 CE
900 CE
1000 CE
1100 CE
1200 CE
1300 CE
1400 CE
1500 CE
1600 CE
1700 CE
1800 CE
1900 CE
2000 CE
2100 CE

Scripture: 2 Kings 2:1-15a,23-25

Suggested Key Verse: 2 Kings 2:23b [23b] Along the way some boys started making fun of him by shouting, "Go away, baldy! Get out of here!"

Suggested Key People: Elijah, Elisha, the boys.

What does this story tell the youth of today? We need to know the context of these stories and questions. We need to know our beliefs. We need to live our lives so that our responses have credibility and honor. Should we make fun of others because of their looks? Should we taunt others for their beliefs or be better prepared to discuss our beliefs? How would you explain this story? Discuss "cursed…in the name of the Lord."

Lesson Summary:

2 Kings 2:1-3 Elijah is planning to leave; Elisha promises to never leave him.

2 Kings 2:4-6 Elijah is going to visit several places before he leaves. Elisha again promises to stay with him and never leave.

2 Kings 2:7-10 Elisha asks Elijah for twice as much power as the other prophets when Elijah leaves.

2 Kings 2:11-15a Elijah leaves suddenly in a flaming chariot pulled by fiery horses. Elisha tears his clothes in sorrow. He strikes the Jordan River with Elijah's coat which has fallen off, wondering if the Lord would work miracles for him as he did for Elijah. A path opens in the river and Elisha walks across.

2 Kings 2:23-25 Later Elisha leaves the area. Along the way some boys start making fun of him. Elisha turns around, stares at the boys, and curses them in the name of the Lord. Two bears run out of the woods and rip 42 of the boys to pieces.

Leader's Research and Student Notes.

_____

_____

_____

_____

_____

_____

_____

_____

_____

_____

_____

_____

_____

_____

_____

_____

_____

_____

_____

_____

Beliefs, Thoughts, Drawings, Scribbles, Doodles.

LESSON 24: Elisha Brings Boy Back to Life

Pre-1500
1500 BC
1400 BC
1300 BC
1200 BC
1100 BC
1000 BC
900 BC
800 BC
700 BC
600 BC
500 BC
400 BC
300 BC
200 BC
100 BC
Christian Era
100 CE
200 CE
300 CE
400 CE
500 CE
600 CE
700 CE
800 CE
900 CE
1000 CE
1100 CE
1200 CE
1300 CE
1400 CE
1500 CE
1600 CE
1700 CE
1800 CE
1900 CE
2000 CE
2100 CE

Scripture: 2 Kings 4:8-37

Suggested Key Verse: 2 Kings 4:17b 17bShe gave birth to a son, just as Elisha had promised."

Suggested Key People: Elisha, rich woman, her son, Gehazi.

What does this story tell the youth of today? Appreciate help when you receive it; offer help when you can. What do you think the son was told as he grew older? What do you think the woman and her husband believed – and told others – as the son grew older? Elisha was known as a prophet of the Lord. Did that affect all of these actions and future actions? Believe that miracles can happen. Trust and have faith in God in your life.

Lesson Summary:

2 Kings 4:8-10 Elisha is entertained while traveling by a rich woman and her husband. They provide a room for him when traveling.

2 Kings 4:11-13 Elisha wishes to do something for the family.

2 Kings 4:14-17 Gehazi tells Elisha that the woman has no son. Elisha promises a son for the woman.

2 Kings 4:18-30 Woman's son becomes ill while in the fields with his father and dies. The woman goes to see Elisha for his help. Elisha tells his servant Gehazi to go help. But the woman won't return home without Elisha.

2 Kings 4:31-37 Elisha gets up and goes with the woman and Gehazi to the woman's house. Elisha heals the son.

Leader's Research and Student Notes.

_____

_____

_____

_____

_____

_____

_____

_____

_____

_____

_____

_____

_____

_____

_____

_____

_____

_____

_____

_____

_____

Beliefs, Thoughts, Drawings, Scribbles, Doodles.

LESSON 25: Naaman and the Servant Girl

Pre-1500
1500 BC
1400 BC
1300 BC
1200 BC
1100 BC
1000 BC
900 BC
800 BC
700 BC
600 BC
500 BC
400 BC
300 BC
200 BC
100 BC
Christian Era
100 CE
200 CE
300 CE
400 CE
500 CE
600 CE
700 CE
800 CE
900 CE
1000 CE
1100 CE
1200 CE
1300 CE
1400 CE
1500 CE
1600 CE
1700 CE
1800 CE
1900 CE
2000 CE
2100 CE

Scripture: 2 Kings 5:1-15

Suggested Key Verse: 2 Kings 5:15a [15a] Naaman and his officials went back to Elisha. Naaman stood in front of him and announced, "Now I know that the God of Israel is the only God in the whole world."

Suggested Key People: Naaman; Naaman's wife; servant of the wife; Naaman's servants; Elisha; king of Israel.

What does this story tell the youth of today? Speak your beliefs; miracles can happen. Our God is God of the entire world. Some solutions are easy, just follow your beliefs (servant girl). Pride was almost Naaman's undoing; don't worry about what you can't (or don't think) you can do. Naaman's gift from God is a perfect example of the New Testament's free gift of our salvation. Accepting that free gift doesn't have to be hard and involved.

Lesson Summary:

2 Kings 5:1-5a Naaman, a brave soldier, has leprosy. An Israelite servant girl suggests he go to the prophet in Samaria who will cure his leprosy.

2 Kings 5:5b-7 Naaman travels with gifts to the Israelite king but the king is afraid.

2 Kings 5:8-10 Elisha the prophet hears about it. He sends someone outside to meet Naaman and recommend a cure by washing seven times in the Jordan River.

2 Kings 5:11-13 Naaman storms off - Elisha didn't even talk to him - and rejects the cure. He thinks other rivers in Damascus would do just as well. His servants question his choice and say that maybe the simple recommendation should be followed.

2 Kings 5:14-15a Naaman changes his mind, follows Elisha's instructions and is cured. He acknowledges the God of Israel as the only God in the whole world.

Leader's Research and Student Notes.

_____

_____

_____

_____

_____

_____

_____

_____

_____

_____

_____

_____

_____

_____

_____

_____

_____

_____

_____

Beliefs, Thoughts, Drawings, Scribbles, Doodles.

LESSON 26: King Joash

Pre-1500
1500 BC
1400 BC
1300 BC
1200 BC
1100 BC
1000 BC
900 BC
800 BC
700 BC
600 BC
500 BC
400 BC
300 BC
200 BC
100 BC
Christian Era
100 CE
200 CE
300 CE
400 CE
500 CE
600 CE
700 CE
800 CE
900 CE
1000 CE
1100 CE
1200 CE
1300 CE
1400 CE
1500 CE
1600 CE
1700 CE
1800 CE
1900 CE
2000 CE
2100 CE

Scripture: 2 Kings 11-12, 2 Chronicles 22-24 (Various verses)

Suggested Key Verse: 2 Chronicles 23:16 [16] Jehoiada asked King Joash and the people to join with him in being faithful to the Lord. They agreed.

Suggested Key People: Queen Athalia, Joash, Jehoiada the priest, Zechariah son of Jehoiada.

What does this story tell the youth of today? Things change; sometimes you have control, sometimes you don't. Be careful of advice given and taken. Choose your friends and mentors carefully. God is in control. Originally Joash was faithful to the Lord; later he turned from God. What causes that to happen? What outside influences can affect your beliefs? How much do you learn and apply from what you hear from family, friends, and others?

Lesson Summary:

2 Chronicles 22:1-7a Death of King Ahaziah and all his sons except Joash put to death.

2 Kings 11:1-3 Joash is rescued just as he was about to be murdered.

2 Kings 11:4b-12 Jehoiada the priest crowns Joash as king and protects him from the Queen.

2 Kings 11:13-16 Queen Athaliah put to death.

2 Chronicles 23:16-21 Joash asks the people to join him in being faithful to the Lord; everyone celebrates; Jerusalem is peaceful again.

2 Chronicles 24:14b-27 Jehoiada the priest dies; Joash turns from God; Zechariah son of Jehoiada is killed; death of Joash.

Leader's Research and Student Notes.

_____

_____

_____

_____

_____

_____

_____

_____

_____

_____

_____

_____

_____

_____

_____

_____

_____

_____

_____

_____

_____

_____

Beliefs, Thoughts, Drawings, Scribbles, Doodles.

LESSON 27: Jeremiah

Pre-1500
1500 BC
1400 BC
1300 BC
1200 BC
1100 BC
1000 BC
900 BC
800 BC
700 BC
600 BC
500 BC
400 BC
300 BC
200 BC
100 BC
Christian Era
100 CE
200 CE
300 CE
400 CE
500 CE
600 CE
700 CE
800 CE
900 CE
1000 CE
1100 CE
1200 CE
1300 CE
1400 CE
1500 CE
1600 CE
1700 CE
1800 CE
1900 CE
2000 CE
2100 CE

Scripture: Jeremiah 1; 18:1-10; 29:10-14; 33:14-16

Suggested Key Verse: Jeremiah 1:5 [5]"Jeremiah, I am your Creator, and before you were born, I chose you to speak for me to the nations."

Suggested Key People: The Lord and Jeremiah.

What does this story tell the youth of today? Jeremiah was probably a teenager or in his early 20's when chosen by the Lord. The Lord says he was chosen to speak before he was born. Does God have plans for all of us before we were born? If yes, when do you think you will know? If not, why not? We can't always answer these questions but we can trust in the Lord to use us as he wants or needs. Trust in and act on your beliefs. Listen to trusted leaders. Have faith that God is always present in your life whether chosen for a very special purpose or not.

Lesson Summary:

Jeremiah 1:4-5 The Lord chooses Jeremiah to speak for him as a prophet.

Jeremiah 1:6-9 Jeremiah argues with the Lord; the Lord promises to help him with what he says and to be with him.

Jeremiah 1:13-16 The Lord shows Jeremiah what is going to happen.

Jeremiah 1:17-19 The Lord again promises to help and protect Jeremiah.

Jeremiah 18:1-10 The Lord sends Jeremiah to a pottery shop for a lesson.

Jeremiah 29:10-14 The Lord promises a blessed future for the nation of Israel.

Jeremiah 33:14-16 The Lord's wonderful promise for Judah and Jerusalem.

Leader's Research and Student Notes.

_____

_____

_____

_____

_____

_____

_____

_____

_____

_____

_____

_____

_____

_____

_____

_____

_____

_____

_____

_____

_____

Beliefs, Thoughts, Drawings, Scribbles, Doodles.

LESSON 28: Daniel

Pre-1500
1500 BC
1400 BC
1300 BC
1200 BC
1100 BC
1000 BC
900 BC
800 BC
700 BC
600 BC
500 BC
400 BC
300 BC
200 BC
100 BC
Christian Era
100 CE
200 CE
300 CE
400 CE
500 CE
600 CE
700 CE
800 CE
900 CE
1000 CE
1100 CE
1200 CE
1300 CE
1400 CE
1500 CE
1600 CE
1700 CE
1800 CE
1900 CE
2000 CE
2100 CE

Scripture: Daniel 1-2, 6 (Various verses)

Suggested Key Verse: Daniel 6:26-27a [26]"I command everyone in my kingdom to worship and honor the God of Daniel. He is the living God, the one who lives forever. His power and his kingdom will never end. [27]He rescues people and sets them free by working great miracles."

Suggested Key People: Daniel, King Nebuchadnezzar, King Darius

What does this story tell the youth of today? Daniel was a youth when selected to serve the King. He was probably from Jewish nobility. Did God have a plan for Daniel when he was selected? God is in control of human events. Every single event? God does care for individuals who are faithful. Can you talk to God when you need help? Do you? Do you trust that God is with you? Does God set us "free" – maybe not spectacularly like Daniel but maybe from other things in our lives?

Lesson Summary:

Daniel 1:3-5 Daniel and others are chosen from among Jewish families to be court officials for the King of Babylon. These young men must be handsome, healthy, smart, wise, educated and fit to serve.

Daniel 1:17-21 God makes Daniel healthy, smart, wise and well-educated to meet the requirements of a court official.

Daniel 2:1-19 King Nebuchadnezzar has nightmares and cannot sleep. He asks advisors to explain them; they cannot. Daniel hears about the dreams and asks God to help.

Daniel 2:24-30 Nebuchadnezzar talks to Daniel and Daniel explains the dreams.

Daniel 2:46-48a The King acknowledges Daniel's God is above all other gods and kings.

Daniel 6:5-9 Later King Darius creates a law that only he can be worshipped. Daniel does not worship the King and continues to worship the Lord.

Daniel 6:16-23 Daniel is thrown to the lions and is rescued by angel; Darius is relieved.

Daniel 6:26-27 The King commands everyone in his kingdom to worship and honor the God of Daniel.

Leader's Research and Student Notes.

_____

_____

_____

_____

_____

_____

_____

_____

_____

_____

_____

_____

_____

_____

_____

_____

Beliefs, Thoughts, Drawings, Scribbles, Doodles.

LESSON 29: Shadrach, Meshach, Abednego

Pre-1500
1500 BC
1400 BC
1300 BC
1200 BC
1100 BC
1000 BC
900 BC
800 BC
700 BC
600 BC
500 BC
400 BC
300 BC
200 BC
100 BC
Christian Era
100 CE
200 CE
300 CE
400 CE
500 CE
600 CE
700 CE
800 CE
900 CE
1000 CE
1100 CE
1200 CE
1300 CE
1400 CE
1500 CE
1600 CE
1700 CE
1800 CE
1900 CE
2000 CE
2100 CE

Scripture: Daniel 3

Suggested Key Verse: Daniel 3: 16-18 [16] The three men replied, "Your Majesty, we don't need to defend ourselves. [17] The God we worship can save us from you and your flaming furnace. [18] But even if he doesn't, we still won't worship your gods and the gold statue you have set up."

Suggested Key People: King Nebuchadnezzar; Shadrach, Meshach, Abednego

What does this story tell the youth of today? Define "worship" as used in this lesson. Surround yourself with good friends. Your actions, beliefs, and way of living can affect others. Does peer pressure affect your decisions? Are your decisions affected by families or others in authority? Believe and trust in God.

Lesson Summary:

Daniel 3:1-6 King Nebuchadnezzar orders a gold statue. He commands all officials to attend its dedication. The officials announce that all must bow down and worship the statue when special music is played.

Daniel 3:8-12 The officials use this announcement as an opportunity to accuse the three Jews - Shadrach, Meshach, and Abednego - of disobeying. (See Lesson 28).

Daniel 3:13-15 King Nebuchadnezzar is furious and gives them one more chance.

Daniel 3:16-18 The three men reply that they do not need to defend themselves. They claim that their God can save them but, in any case, they will not worship Nebuchadnezzar.

Daniel 3:19-23 They are thrown into the fiery furnace that has been heated seven times hotter than usual. The King sees that Shadrach, Meshach and Abednego are not harmed.

Daniel 3:24-30 The King sees that the three men are accompanied in the furnace by another and all are OK. He removes them from the furnace and praises their God.

Leader's Research and Student Notes.

_____

_____

_____

_____

_____

_____

_____

_____

_____

_____

_____

_____

_____

_____

_____

_____

_____

Beliefs, Thoughts, Drawings, Scribbles, Doodles.

LESSON 30: Esther

Scripture: Esther 1-10 (Various verses)

Suggested Key Verse: Esther 4:13-14 [13]he (Mordecai) sent back this reply (to Esther), "Don't think that you will escape being killed with the rest of the Jews, just because you live in the king's palace. [14]If you don't speak up now, we will somehow get help, but you and your family will be killed. It could be that you were made queen for a time like this!"

Suggested Key People: Esther, Mordecai, King Xerxes, Haman

What does this story tell the youth of today? God cares and will be with his people. Esther was very young when taken to be with the King, maybe younger than 14. How did this affect her? With God's help could you handle new situations as Esther did? You may be asked to make some small (or large) statement for Christ. Your situation may offer a place to significantly affect others. Do not worry about current problems or challenges, trust in the Lord.

Lesson Summary:

Esther 1:1-22 King Xerxes is irritated by Queen Vashti and removes her as Queen.

Esther 2:1-4 King Xerxes starts a search for some beautiful young women in his kingdom. The young women are to be given beauty treatments and the King's favorite to be made queen.

Esther 2:5-23 Esther, raised by her cousin/uncle Mordecai, is chosen as new queen but does not reveal her Jewish heritage. Mordecai discovers a plot against the king.

Esther 3:1-15 Haman is appointed as the King's viceroy. Mordecai irritates Haman and in revenge Haman plots to kill Mordecai and all the Jews in the empire.

Esther 4:1-5:14 Mordecai discovers the plot and asks Esther to intercede with the King.

Esther 6:1-11 King Xerxes cannot sleep. He stays awake reviewing court records that reveal that Mordecai had saved his life.

Esther 7:1-10 King Xerxes and Haman attend Esther's second banquet and the King promises to grant Esther any request she would make.

Esther 8:1-10:3 King Xerxes is angry and modifies his earlier decree to kill the Jews. He allows the Jews to destroy all of those seeking to kill them.

Leader's Research and Student Notes.

_____

_____

_____

_____

_____

_____

_____

_____

_____

_____

_____

_____

_____

Beliefs, Thoughts, Drawings, Scribbles, Doodles.

LESSON 31: John the Baptist

Pre-1500
1500 BC
1400 BC
1300 BC
1200 BC
1100 BC
1000 BC
900 BC
800 BC
700 BC
600 BC
500 BC
400 BC
300 BC
200 BC
100 BC
Christian Era
100 CE
200 CE
300 CE
400 CE
500 CE
600 CE
700 CE
800 CE
900 CE
1000 CE
1100 CE
1200 CE
1300 CE
1400 CE
1500 CE
1600 CE
1700 CE
1800 CE
1900 CE
2000 CE
2100 CE

Scripture: Luke 1 (Various verses)

Suggested Key Verse: Luke 1:16-17 [16] John will lead many people in Israel to turn back to the Lord their God. [17] He will go ahead of the Lord with the same power and spirit that Elijah had. And because of John, parents will be more thoughtful of their children. And people who now disobey God will begin to think as they ought to. This is how John will get people ready for the Lord.

Suggested Key People: John, Zechariah, Elizabeth, the angel.

What does this story tell the youth of today? John was chosen by God before he was even born. His parents knew this. Did that affect the life he lived before his ministry? Does that still happen today? Some people know their beliefs and life's work at an early age. John had faith in his calling. Could you be called – maybe even in minor things that you don't think of? Do you live as if your life is for Christ? The last part of the key verse says that "parents will be more thoughtful... and people who now disobey God will begin to think as they ought to." Do you believe that is true today?

Lesson Summary:

Luke 1:5-10 Luke tells the background of Zechariah and Elizabeth, John's parents. Zechariah, a priest, was performing his duties at the temple. His wife could not have children.

Luke 1:11-17 An angel appears to Zechariah and promises him a son who will be a great servant of the Lord.

Luke 1:18-22 Zechariah has doubts but the angel tells Zechariah he will not be able to talk until the child is born. The crowd in the temple realize that Zechariah has seen a vision.

Luke 1:23-25,57-64 John is born and taken to the temple as required. Zechariah writes John's name on a tablet and regains his voice.

Luke 1:65-66 The neighbors are frightened and people are talking. They know that God is with John.

Luke 1:80 As he grew up, God's spirit gave John great power. John lived in the desert until he was sent to the people of Israel.

Leader's Research and Student Notes.

_____

_____

_____

_____

_____

_____

_____

_____

_____

_____

_____

_____

_____

_____

_____

_____

Beliefs, Thoughts, Drawings, Scribbles, Doodles.

LESSON 32: Mary - Prophesies about Her Life

Pre-1500
1500 BC
1400 BC
1300 BC
1200 BC
1100 BC
1000 BC
900 BC
800 BC
700 BC
600 BC
500 BC
400 BC
300 BC
200 BC
100 BC
Christian Era
100 CE
200 CE
300 CE
400 CE
500 CE
600 CE
700 CE
800 CE
900 CE
1000 CE
1100 CE
1200 CE
1300 CE
1400 CE
1500 CE
1600 CE
1700 CE
1800 CE
1900 CE
2000 CE
2100 CE

Scripture: Luke 1:26-45; Luke 2:25-35

Suggested Key Verse: Luke 1:28 [28] The angel greeted Mary and said, "You are truly blessed! The Lord is with you." Luke 2:35a [35]"...you, Mary, will suffer as though you had been stabbed by a dagger."

Suggested Key People: Mary, Elizabeth, angel, Simeon.

What does this story tell the youth of today? Mary hears two prophesies about her son and her life – she is blessed because the Lord is with her and that she will suffer as if she were stabbed. Does your life sometime seem this way – very high or extremely low, sometimes with no real reason? Don't expect everything to be perfect in your life. Highs and lows come to everyone regardless of age. Listen for God's call. Trust him to help you through both. God is always near and in control - by His definition but maybe not yours. He is here for us all, all the time.

Lesson Summary:

Luke 1:26-38 Mary is engaged to Joseph from the family of King David. But she is not yet married. An angel tells Mary that she is blessed and will have a son named Jesus to be called the holy Son of God.

Luke 1:39-45 Mary visits with her relative, Elizabeth, who is also expecting a special child to be known as John the Baptist.

Luke 2:25-28 Later Mary and Joseph take baby Jesus to the temple to follow the Law of Moses and there they meet Simeon. Simeon was a good man waiting for God to save the people of Israel.

Luke 2:29-32 Simeon praises God because God has kept his promise of a savior.

Luke 2:33-35 Simeon blesses Mary and Joseph and warns Mary of the future for her and for Jesus.

Leader's Research and Student Notes.

_____

_____

_____

_____

_____

_____

_____

_____

_____

_____

_____

_____

_____

_____

_____

_____

_____

_____

_____

_____

_____

_____

Beliefs, Thoughts, Drawings, Scribbles, Doodles.

LESSON 33: Jesus in the Temple

Pre-1500
1500 BC
1400 BC
1300 BC
1200 BC
1100 BC
1000 BC
900 BC
800 BC
700 BC
600 BC
500 BC
400 BC
300 BC
200 BC
100 BC
Christian Era
100 CE
200 CE
300 CE
400 CE
500 CE
600 CE
700 CE
800 CE
900 CE
1000 CE
1100 CE
1200 CE
1300 CE
1400 CE
1500 CE
1600 CE
1700 CE
1800 CE
1900 CE
2000 CE
2100 CE

Scripture: Luke 2:41-52

Suggested Key Verse: Luke 2:52 [52] Jesus became wise, and he grew strong. God was pleased with him and so were the people.

Suggested Key People: Jesus, Mary, Joseph

What does this story tell the youth of today? It is hard to compare yourself to Jesus. However, you are never too young to talk about and practice your faith. Do you study and learn from the Bible and other practices such as attending church, youth groups, summer camps? In the current day and age, do you use online options to study, worship, and grow your faith? Do you discuss your faith with peers, teachers, or family? Others may learn from you. Do you try to please people for the wrong reasons? With the wrong actions? You should show respect for your parents and love for God.

Lesson Summary:

Luke 2:41-45 When he is 12, Jesus takes a trip to Jerusalem for Passover with his parents. After Passover, his parents left, assuming that Jesus was with friends on the trip home. But he had stayed in Jerusalem.

Luke 2:46-47 Three days later Jesus is found in the temple, listening to the teachers, and asking questions. Everyone was surprised at how much he knew.

Luke 2:48-50 Jesus' parents are amazed. They ask why he stayed behind. Jesus explains about his "father's house" but they do not understand what he means.

Luke 2:51-52 Jesus grows and becomes wise and strong. He obeys his parents. God is pleased with him and so are the people.

Leader's Research and Student Notes.

_____

_____

_____

_____

_____

_____

_____

_____

_____

_____

_____

_____

_____

_____

_____

_____

_____

_____

_____

_____

_____

_____

_____

_____

Beliefs, Thoughts, Drawings, Scribbles, Doodles.

LESSON 34: Jairus' Daughter

Pre-1500
1500 BC
1400 BC
1300 BC
1200 BC
1100 BC
1000 BC
900 BC
800 BC
700 BC
600 BC
500 BC
400 BC
300 BC
200 BC
100 BC
Christian Era
100 CE
200 CE
300 CE
400 CE
500 CE
600 CE
700 CE
800 CE
900 CE
1000 CE
1100 CE
1200 CE
1300 CE
1400 CE
1500 CE
1600 CE
1700 CE
1800 CE
1900 CE
2000 CE
2100 CE

Scripture: Luke 8:40-56

Suggested Key Verse: Luke 8:50a [50a] When Jesus heard this, he told Jairus, "Don't worry! Have faith, and your daughter will get well."

Suggested Key People: Jesus, Jairus, Jairus' daughter.

What does this story tell the youth of today? These verses are very short with two different people being healed in two different situations. Jairus begged; the woman said she had just touched Jesus. But both healings were accomplished because Jesus recognized the requestor's faith. Have faith, study. When you have doubts ask for help to believe from others you trust. Pray. Ask for help when you need it - but don't demand the results you want. God is aware of your needs. Why did Jesus tell the parents not to tell anyone? One commentary suggests that Jesus did not want people focusing on the miracles, but to focus on the message He proclaimed and the death He was going to die.

Lesson Summary:

Luke 8:40-42a Jairus begs Jesus to come to his home and help because his 12-year old daughter is dying.

Luke 8:42b-48 On his way to Jairus' home, Jesus heals a woman because of her faith. She said that she had touched Jesus and she had been healed at once.

Luke 8:49-50 Jairus' daughter dies while Jesus continues to her home. Jesus tells Jairus not to worry and to have faith because his daughter will get well.

Luke 8:51-56 Jesus goes into the house with Peter, John, James and the girl's parents. Everyone was crying but Jesus said that the girl was just sleeping. He heals Jairus' daughter and orders the parents not to tell anyone.

Leader's Research and Student Notes.

_____

_____

_____

_____

_____

_____

_____

_____

_____

_____

_____

_____

_____

_____

_____

_____

_____

_____

_____

_____

_____

_____

Beliefs, Thoughts, Drawings, Scribbles, Doodles.

LESSON 35: Boy with a Demon

Pre-1500
1500 BC
1400 BC
1300 BC
1200 BC
1100 BC
1000 BC
900 BC
800 BC
700 BC
600 BC
500 BC
400 BC
300 BC
200 BC
100 BC
Christian Era
100 CE
200 CE
300 CE
400 CE
500 CE
600 CE
700 CE
800 CE
900 CE
1000 CE
1100 CE
1200 CE
1300 CE
1400 CE
1500 CE
1600 CE
1700 CE
1800 CE
1900 CE
2000 CE
2100 CE

Scripture: Luke 9:37-48

Suggested Key Verse: Luke 9:41b [41b] "...Why do I have to put up with you?"

Suggested Key People: Jesus, son and father, disciples.

What does this story tell the youth of today? Do you believe in demons? What to you is a demon? In the previous lesson, Jairus' daughter was healed because of her father's faith. In this lesson Jesus calls the crowd faithless but heals the son. Do you think that Jesus as a human was sometimes frustrated as we all are? What do you do when you are frustrated? What do you do when you are the person causing the frustration? In either case is the frustration sometimes due to misunderstanding? Did the disciples, just like us although they were there to walk and talk directly with Jesus, have problems understanding Jesus? Have faith; study; learn as much as you can.

Lesson Summary:

Luke 9:37-40 Jesus and his three disciples come down from the mountain. They encounter someone with a hurting son. A demon often attacks the son and won't leave until the boy is completely worn out.

Luke 9:41-42 Jesus calls the crowd stubborn and faithless. He asks to see the son and the demon attacks. Jesus orders the demon to stop and then heals the son and returns him to his father.

Luke 9:43a Everyone is amazed at God's great power.

Luke 9:43b-45 While everyone is still amazed, he tells his disciples to pay attention. He tells them the Son of Man will be handed over to his enemies. But the disciples do not understand and are afraid to ask.

Luke 9:46-48 Jesus' disciples argue about which is the greatest. Jesus talks about welcoming a child in his name because that is the same as welcoming Jesus. He closes this lesson by telling them that the humblest is the greatest.

Leader's Research and Student Notes.

The previous lesson was all about faith. This lesson is also but with a little different slant.

_____

_____

_____

_____

_____

_____

_____

_____

_____

_____

_____

_____

_____

_____

_____

_____

Beliefs, Thoughts, Drawings, Scribbles, Doodles.

LESSON 36: The Prodigal Son

Pre-1500
1500 BC
1400 BC
1300 BC
1200 BC
1100 BC
1000 BC
900 BC
800 BC
700 BC
600 BC
500 BC
400 BC
300 BC
200 BC
100 BC
Christian Era
100 CE
200 CE
300 CE
400 CE
500 CE
600 CE
700 CE
800 CE
900 CE
1000 CE
1100 CE
1200 CE
1300 CE
1400 CE
1500 CE
1600 CE
1700 CE
1800 CE
1900 CE
2000 CE
2100 CE

Scripture: Luke 15:11-32

Suggested Key Verse: Luke 15:24b [24b] "…He was lost and has now been found."

Suggested Key People: Prodigal son, older son, their father.

What does this story tell the youth of today? There is no shame in love. The father always loved both his sons. Our God always loves us. Others, including religious people can make you ashamed. You can make others ashamed. But you can be forgiven and you also can forgive others. Be thankful that our God gives forgiveness and compassion if we are willing to receive them. What finally happened to the older son? Did he forgive? Did the brothers learn a lesson? Did their father help? Have you lost family, friends, or others because you could not forgive? If so, pray for help and understanding.

Lesson Summary:

Luke 15:11-13a In this story from Jesus, a younger son asks for his inheritance. His father divides his property between his sons and the younger son leaves home.

Luke 15:13b-16 The younger son leaves for a foreign country and wastes all his inheritance in wild living. He spends everything he has. There is a famine, and he has nothing to eat.

Luke 15:17-20 Finally he comes to his senses and decides he has made a big mistake. He starts back home. His father recognizes him at a distance and runs to his son.

Luke 15:21-24 The son admits that he has sinned against God and is no longer fit to be called a son. The father welcomes the younger son back with open arms and celebrates.

Luke 15:25-32 Meanwhile the older son is upset even though his father tells him that everything he has belongs to the older son. The father wants to celebrate because the younger son is alive; he was lost but has been found.

Leader's Research and Student Notes.

_____

_____

_____

_____

_____

_____

_____

_____

_____

_____

_____

_____

_____

_____

_____

_____

_____

_____

Beliefs, Thoughts, Drawings, Scribbles, Doodles.

LESSON 37: Daughter of Herodias

Scripture: Mark 6:14-29

Suggested Key Verse: Mark 6:26 [26] Herod was very sorry for what he had said. But he did not want to break the promise he had made in front of his guests.

Suggested Key People: King Herod, Herodias, daughter of Herodias, John the Baptist

What does this story tell the youth of today? John the Baptist was not afraid to say what he believed. It ended up costing him his life. That's a serious belief. But even minor beliefs can result in problems. Stay true to your beliefs regardless of outside pressure; do not cause or encourage others to sin or make bad choices. Surround yourself with people who can support and honor your beliefs. Be careful what you promise and careful what you ask for. Was the daughter innocent of wrongdoing? Did she believe that John was in prison as an enemy of the State and her family? At times you must verify your beliefs; talk to trusted family, advisors, and teachers. Study.

Lesson Summary:

Mark 6:14-16 Jesus becomes so well known that Herod the ruler hears of him. Herod exclaims that it must be John by another name and that he had had his head cut off.

Mark 6:17-20 Earlier Herod had married his brother's wife, Herodias. John told him it wasn't right so Herod had John thrown in prison.

Mark 6:21-23 Later at Herod's birthday party, the daughter of Herodias danced for Herod and Herod's guests at the party. She pleased Herod so much that he made a rash promise to give her anything she asked for up to half of his kingdom.

Mark 6:24-25 After dancing she left the party and asked her mother what gift she should request. Her mother, Herodias, told her to ask Herod for the head of John the Baptist.

Mark 6:26-29 King Herod was sorry for what he had said but unwilling to break a promise made in front of his party guests. At once a guard was ordered to cut off John's head in the prison. John was beheaded and Herod gave the daughter John's head on a platter who gave it to her mother. John's followers learned that he had been killed. They took the body and put it in a tomb.

Leader's Research and Student Notes.

_____

_____

_____

_____

_____

_____

_____

_____

_____

_____

_____

_____

_____

_____

_____

Beliefs, Thoughts, Drawings, Scribbles, Doodles.

LESSON 38: A Canaanite Woman's Faith

Pre-1500
1500 BC
1400 BC
1300 BC
1200 BC
1100 BC
1000 BC
900 BC
800 BC
700 BC
600 BC
500 BC
400 BC
300 BC
200 BC
100 BC
Christian Era
100 CE
200 CE
300 CE
400 CE
500 CE
600 CE
700 CE
800 CE
900 CE
1000 CE
1100 CE
1200 CE
1300 CE
1400 CE
1500 CE
1600 CE
1700 CE
1800 CE
1900 CE
2000 CE
2100 CE

Scripture: Matthew 15:21-28

Suggested Key Verse: Matthew 15:28a ²⁸ᵃJesus answered, "Dear woman, you really do have a lot of faith, and you will be given what you want."

Suggested Key People: Jesus, Canaanite woman, daughter of Canaanite woman.

What does this story tell the youth of today? Note: An interesting and disturbing scripture. Just before this story Jesus and his disciples had just tried to withdraw from religious leaders and crowds. Soon after this story he continues to another highly Gentile area and heals many. Lots of words attributed to Jesus to discuss: "I was sent only to the people of Israel", "flock of lost sheep", "take food...feed it to the dogs", "crumbs". Jesus walked away originally without talking to the woman. Later he acknowledged her strong faith. Was the daughter old enough to understand her demon or what Jesus did? What will the daughter be told as she grows older? Will she share the message of faith and healing? Will she tell about Jesus? Was this a teaching moment for the disciples? Was this the human side of a very tired Jesus?

Lesson Summary:

Matthew 15:21-23 A Canaanite woman comes out shouting at Jesus for pity. Her daughter is full of demons. Jesus does not answer. The woman follows and continues shouting. His disciples come up and ask Jesus to send her away.

Matthew 15:24 Jesus says he was sent to the people of Israel who are like lost sheep.

Matthew 15:25-27 The woman begs. Jesus talks about taking food away from children and feeding it to the dogs. The woman says that even puppies get crumbs from the owner's table.

Matthew 15:28 Jesus responds to the woman's faith and gives her what she wants. Her daughter is healed.

Leader's Research and Student Notes.

_____

_____

_____

_____

_____

_____

_____

_____

_____

_____

_____

_____

_____

_____

_____

_____

_____

_____

_____

_____

Beliefs, Thoughts, Drawings, Scribbles, Doodles.

LESSON 39: Ten Young Women

Pre-1500
1500 BC
1400 BC
1300 BC
1200 BC
1100 BC
1000 BC
900 BC
800 BC
700 BC
600 BC
500 BC
400 BC
300 BC
200 BC
100 BC
Christian Era
100 CE
200 CE
300 CE
400 CE
500 CE
600 CE
700 CE
800 CE
900 CE
1000 CE
1100 CE
1200 CE
1300 CE
1400 CE
1500 CE
1600 CE
1700 CE
1800 CE
1900 CE
2000 CE
2100 CE

Scripture: Matthew 25:1-13

Suggested Key Verse: Matthew 25:13 [13] So, my disciples, always be ready! You don't know the day or the time when all this will happen.

Suggested Key People: Jesus and his disciples, bridegroom, ten young women.

What does this story tell the youth of today? Who does the bridegroom represent? Why was the bridegroom late? Was he late or did the personal expectations of the women not match the plans of the bridegroom? What did the five women who were prepared say to the foolish women? What did the foolish women say? Were they more interested in the bridegroom or the party? Always be ready! Do not live your life foolishly. Live your life at all times prepared for the return of Jesus.

Lesson Summary:

Matthew 25:1-4 This is a parable told by Jesus about ten young women going to a wedding. Five of them are foolish (took no extra oil for their lamps) and five are wise (took extra oil).

Matthew 25:5-6 The bridegroom is late in arriving and the young women fall asleep. In the middle of the night someone shouts that the bridegroom is coming.

Matthew 25:7-9 The women begin getting their lamps ready. The foolish women ask for oil from the wise but there is not enough. They are told to go buy some for themselves.

Matthew 25:10-11 The bridegroom comes but the foolish women are not there. The wise women go in with the bridegroom and the doors are closed. Later the other women arrive and shout for the door to be opened.

Matthew 25:12-13 The bridegroom says he doesn't know the foolish women. At the end of the parable Jesus says to his disciples, "always be ready...".

Leader's Research and Student Notes.

_____

_____

_____

_____

_____

_____

_____

_____

_____

_____

_____

_____

_____

_____

_____

_____

_____

_____

_____

_____

Beliefs, Thoughts, Drawings, Scribbles, Doodles.

LESSON 40: Boy with Fish and Bread

Pre-1500
1500 BC
1400 BC
1300 BC
1200 BC
1100 BC
1000 BC
900 BC
800 BC
700 BC
600 BC
500 BC
400 BC
300 BC
200 BC
100 BC
Christian Era
100 CE
200 CE
300 CE
400 CE
500 CE
600 CE
700 CE
800 CE
900 CE
1000 CE
1100 CE
1200 CE
1300 CE
1400 CE
1500 CE
1600 CE
1700 CE
1800 CE
1900 CE
2000 CE
2100 CE

Scripture: John 6:1-15

Suggested Key Verse: John 6:9 [9] "There is a boy here who has five small loaves of barley bread and two fish. But what good is that with all these people?"

Suggested Key People: Jesus, the boy, Philip, Andrew, the people, the disciples.

What does this story tell the youth of today? We never know which person God will use, and how. We would never think of using a young boy and his small offering. What did the boy think of later? Did he remember Jesus all his life as a follower of his teaching? God knows us all; where we are, what we have, and how we can be used. How does God provide? Directly? In answer to prayer? Through the efforts of other Christians? Through the efforts of others regardless of their religious beliefs? Does God use all of us to help others, regardless of age, sex, wealth, education, etc.? Are miracles still possible today? God may test your beliefs through the needs of others. After the crowd saw Jesus perform this miracle, Jesus went up the mountain to be alone. What did that mean?

Lesson Summary:

John 6:1-4 Jesus has just worked miracles to heal the sick and a large crowd is following him. Jesus goes up a mountain with his disciples and sits down.

John 6:5-7 Jesus sees the large crowd and tests Philip, asking Philip where they can get enough food for all the people. Philip answers with the cost of just a little bread to feed the people.

John 6:8-9 Andrew mentions a boy with five small loaves of bread and two fish but asks what good that would do.

John 6:10-13 Jesus tells everyone to sit down, 5,000 men and others. He takes the bread in his hands and gives thanks to God. Then he passes out the bread and fish. All eat all they want and there is a lot left over.

John 6:14-15 The people who have seen this miracle want to name Jesus as the prophet who was to come. Jesus realizes they would try to force him to be their king. He goes up a mountain to be alone.

Leader's Research and Student Notes.

_____

_____

_____

_____

_____

_____

_____

_____

_____

_____

_____

_____

_____

_____

_____

_____

_____

Beliefs, Thoughts, Drawings, Scribbles, Doodles.

LESSON 41: Rhoda

Pre-1500
1500 BC
1400 BC
1300 BC
1200 BC
1100 BC
1000 BC
900 BC
800 BC
700 BC
600 BC
500 BC
400 BC
300 BC
200 BC
100 BC
Christian Era
100 CE
200 CE
300 CE
400 CE
500 CE
600 CE
700 CE
800 CE
900 CE
1000 CE
1100 CE
1200 CE
1300 CE
1400 CE
1500 CE
1600 CE
1700 CE
1800 CE
1900 CE
2000 CE
2100 CE

Scripture: Acts 12:11-17

Suggested Key Verse: Acts 12:15a [15a] "You are crazy!" everyone told her. But she kept saying it was Peter.

Suggested Key People: Rhoda, Peter, followers of Jesus.

What does this story tell the youth of today? Rhoda is mentioned only once in the bible. Was this servant girl, Rhoda, one of Jesus' followers? Was she praying with the disciples? The followers were praying but they did not accept the answers to their prayers. Rhoda did and carried them the joyful message. God answers prayer: prayers work miracles. Is this particularly true when given the faith of a child? We should always affirm our beliefs even when others tell us we are crazy. Listen for the spirit's voice when in times of stress. Don't leave the spirit standing outside your life at any time. Learn from Rhoda and share the news of what God can do, remaining confident in what you know is true.

Lesson Summary:

Acts 12:11-12 Peter has just been released (escaped?) from prison miraculously, certain that the Lord had sent an angel to his rescue. He then goes to a house where many of Jesus' followers had come together and were praying.

Acts 12:13-14 Peter knocks on the gate and Rhoda comes to answer. She recognizes Peter's voice and is too excited to open the gate. She runs inside to say it is Peter.

Acts 12:15-16 Everyone tells Rhoda she is crazy. But she keeps saying it is Peter. They finally open the gate and are amazed.

Acts 12:17 Peter motions to them to keep quiet. Peter then tells the followers how Jesus led him out of jail and asks them to tell the others. Peter then leaves.

Leader's Research and Student Notes.

_____

_____

_____

_____

_____

_____

_____

_____

_____

_____

_____

_____

_____

_____

_____

_____

_____

_____

_____

_____

_____

Beliefs, Thoughts, Drawings, Scribbles, Doodles.

LESSON 42: Slave Girl and Paul

Pre-1500
1500 BC
1400 BC
1300 BC
1200 BC
1100 BC
1000 BC
900 BC
800 BC
700 BC
600 BC
500 BC
400 BC
300 BC
200 BC
100 BC
Christian Era
100 CE
200 CE
300 CE
400 CE
500 CE
600 CE
700 CE
800 CE
900 CE
1000 CE
1100 CE
1200 CE
1300 CE
1400 CE
1500 CE
1600 CE
1700 CE
1800 CE
1900 CE
2000 CE
2100 CE

Scripture: Acts 16:16-22

Suggested Key Verse: Acts 16:17 [17] The girl followed Paul and the rest of us, and she kept yelling, "These men are servants of the Most High God! They are telling you how to be saved."

Suggested Key People: Paul, slave girl, girl's owners, the crowd, and Roman officials.

What does this story tell the youth of today? The demon-possessed spirit in the girl is saying the truth. Was that on purpose? What was the spirit trying to do? Why did the spirit choose this girl? What happened to the girl later? How did she make a living? Did she return home to her family? We do not know. Try to determine why people act the way they do and react appropriately. Are they slaves to something in today's world? Pray for your discernment and for help for others. Trust in your faith as a Christian. Jesus can change people and make a difference. We can be a tool for Jesus on earth.

Lesson Summary:

Acts 12:16 Paul and Silas are met by a slave girl with a spirit in her that gave her the power to tell the future – and to make a lot of money for her owners.

Acts 12:17-18a The slave girl follows Paul and the rest of the disciples for several days. She keeps yelling about the "Most High God" and "how to be saved."

Acts 12:18b Paul gets very upset. In the name of Jesus Christ, he orders the spirit to leave the girl alone. At once the evil spirit leaves.

Acts 12:19-21 The owners of the slave girl realize they will lose the money they were making and drag Paul and Silas into court. They tell the Roman officials that the men were upsetting the city.

Acts 12:22 Paul and Silas are attacked by the crowd. The officials order them to be beaten with a whip.

Leader's Research and Student Notes.

_____

_____

_____

_____

_____

_____

_____
_____
_____
_____
_____
_____
_____
_____
_____
_____
_____
_____
_____
_____

Beliefs, Thoughts, Drawings, Scribbles, Doodles.

LESSON 43: Eutychus

Pre-1500
1500 BC
1400 BC
1300 BC
1200 BC
1100 BC
1000 BC
900 BC
800 BC
700 BC
600 BC
500 BC
400 BC
300 BC
200 BC
100 BC
Christian Era
100 CE
200 CE
300 CE
400 CE
500 CE
600 CE
700 CE
800 CE
900 CE
1000 CE
1100 CE
1200 CE
1300 CE
1400 CE
1500 CE
1600 CE
1700 CE
1800 CE
1900 CE
2000 CE
2100 CE

Scripture: Acts 20: 3b,6-12

Suggested Key Verse: [10b] "Don't worry! He's alive."

Suggested Key People: Paul, Eutychus, followers of Jesus.

What does this story tell the youth of today? Don't sleep in church or don't preach too long (just kidding). Paul was a true apostle full of signs, wonders, and miracles. Do take advantage of your opportunities to learn more about God's gift to us, his son Jesus. Always be careful; balance what you are doing with what you can do physically and emotionally. Don't devote so much time, even to church and service activities, that you neglect your studies, families, and even time to rest and be alone with the Lord in prayer. God valued Eutychus' life and desire to hear Jesus and brought him back to life through the hands of Paul. What do you think Eutychus remembered about Paul's visit? Was this his first chance to hear about Jesus? Did this change his life?

Lesson Summary:

Acts 20:3b,6 Paul is traveling. Due to a change of plans he ends up meeting friends in Troas.

Acts 20:7-8 Paul and other people meet on the first day of the week to break bread together. They are meeting in an upstairs room with a lot of lamps.

Acts 20:9 A young man, Eutychus, is sitting on a windowsill. While he listens to Paul, Eutychus gets very sleepy. He goes to sleep and falls three floors to the ground. When he is picked up, he is dead.

Acts 20:10 Paul goes down, takes Eutychus in his arms, and tells the other not to worry – that Eutychus is not dead.

Acts 20:11-12 Paul and others break bread and eat together. Paul then speaks until dawn and leaves Troas. The followers take the young man home alive and happy.

Leader's Research and Student Notes.

_____

_____

_____

_____

_____

_____

_____

_____

_____

_____

_____

_____

_____

_____

_____

_____

_____

_____

_____

_____

Beliefs, Thoughts, Drawings, Scribbles, Doodles.

LESSON 44: Paul's Nephew

Pre-1500
1500 BC
1400 BC
1300 BC
1200 BC
1100 BC
1000 BC
900 BC
800 BC
700 BC
600 BC
500 BC
400 BC
300 BC
200 BC
100 BC
Christian Era
100 CE
200 CE
300 CE
400 CE
500 CE
600 CE
700 CE
800 CE
900 CE
1000 CE
1100 CE
1200 CE
1300 CE
1400 CE
1500 CE
1600 CE
1700 CE
1800 CE
1900 CE
2000 CE
2100 CE

Scripture: Acts 23:12-22

Suggested Key Verse: Acts 23:16 [16] When Paul's nephew heard about the plot, he went to the fortress and told Paul about it.

Suggested Key People: Paul's nephew; Paul; the commander of the fortress; Jewish leaders and men.

What does this story tell the youth of today? Paul wrote 13 (or 14) of the books in the New Testament. Without the actions of his nephew, we might not have much of the New Testament. Probably his nephew never knew this. What effect do you think this incident had on the nephew? Did he learn more as he grew older? Did he later tell family or friends about the plot? Sometimes you will be in a position that you do not like. That may be a coincidence or part of God's plan for your life. You may be asked to leave your comfort zone. You may need the courage to follow your beliefs or your faith. In some situations, keeping secrets may be asked of you. Your life is important and your interactions with others are important. Help others when you can. Do not let fear overcome love. Trust in God to always be with you.

Lesson Summary:

Acts 23:12-15 Forty Jewish men get together and vow not to eat or drink until they have killed Paul. They then go to the nation's leaders and reveal their promise. They want Paul to be brought to court so that they can kill him on the way.

Acts 23:16-18 Paul's nephew hears about the plot, notifies his uncle Paul, and Paul sends the nephew to speak to the commander of the fortress.

Acts 23:19-21 The commander hears about the plot from Paul's nephew and listens to the details.

Acts 23:22 The commander sends the nephew away and advises him to keep silent about the plot.

Leader's Research and Student Notes.

_____

_____

_____

_____

_____

_____

_____

_____

_____

_____

_____

_____

_____

_____

_____

_____

_____

_____

Beliefs, Thoughts, Drawings, Scribbles, Doodles.

LESSON 45: Paul on the Island of Malta

Pre-1500
1500 BC
1400 BC
1300 BC
1200 BC
1100 BC
1000 BC
900 BC
800 BC
700 BC
600 BC
500 BC
400 BC
300 BC
200 BC
100 BC
Christian Era
100 CE
200 CE
300 CE
400 CE
500 CE
600 CE
700 CE
800 CE
900 CE
1000 CE
1100 CE
1200 CE
1300 CE
1400 CE
1500 CE
1600 CE
1700 CE
1800 CE
1900 CE
2000 CE
2100 CE

Scripture: Acts 28:1-11

Suggested Key Verse: Acts 28:5 [5] Paul shook the snake off into the fire and wasn't harmed.

Suggested Key People: Paul and his shipmates; the people of Malta.

What does this story tell the youth of today? Note: Per one report, Malta is alone among current nations as having a 2,000-year-old Christian tradition. This is one of the few stories in this series that does not directly involve youth at all. The story occurs just after Paul was shipwrecked on the island on his trip to Rome as a prisoner. It is a good time to talk about Paul and his ministry, challenges, and final trip to Rome. This story can lead to some good discussions about the effects that Paul had on the youth of Malta and what the long-term results of learning at that age can be. Could they and did they apply what they learned from Paul's visit for the rest of their lives? Do you learn from your Christian studies? Do you apply the lessons you learn?

Lesson Summary:

Acts 28:1-2 After many trials on his journey to Rome, Paul and his shipmates come ashore on Malta. The local people are very friendly.

Acts 28:3-5 Trying to warm up, Paul collects wood for a fire and is bitten by a snake. The people of Malta believe he is being punished by the goddess of justice.

Acts 28:6 The people think he will drop dead. They watch him for a long time but nothing happens. They then decide he is a god.

Acts 28:7-8 Paul becomes friendly with the governor and heals the governor's father by praying and placing his hands on him.

Acts 28:9-11 Paul heals many sick people. He is respected by the people of Malta. He and his shipmates are given everything they need before leaving for Rome.

Leader's Research and Student Notes.

_____

_____

_____

_____

_____

_____

_____

_____

_____

_____

_____

_____

_____

_____

_____

_____

_____

_____

_____

_____

_____

Beliefs, Thoughts, Drawings, Scribbles, Doodles.

LESSON 46: Young People

Pre-1500
1500 BC
1400 BC
1300 BC
1200 BC
1100 BC
1000 BC
900 BC
800 BC
700 BC
600 BC
500 BC
400 BC
300 BC
200 BC
100 BC
Christian Era
100 CE
200 CE
300 CE
400 CE
500 CE
600 CE
700 CE
800 CE
900 CE
1000 CE
1100 CE
1200 CE
1300 CE
1400 CE
1500 CE
1600 CE
1700 CE
1800 CE
1900 CE
2000 CE
2100 CE

Scripture: 1 Peter 5:5-8

Suggested Key Verse: 1 Peter 5:7 [7] God cares for you, so turn all your worries over to him.

Suggested Key People: Peter (traditionally the Apostle Peter).

What does this story tell the youth of today? In these verses, Peter might be talking to the young people who are active in the young churches, not necessarily to youth as we understand our current culture. But the message is the same – obey your elders, be humble to others and to God. He emphasizes that God cares for all and that we should share our worries with him. Do you share with God? Do you share more than your worries? Do you think he wants to hear from you – good or bad, just like your earthly family wants to talk with you? Are your prayers "scheduled" to a certain time and place on certain days of the week? Can you talk with God any time without a special appointment? Do you?

Lesson Summary:

1 Peter 5:5 Peter instructs young people to obey their elders and be humble toward everyone else.

1 Peter 5:6 He says to be humble in the presence of God's mighty power and that God will honor you when the time comes.

1 Peter 5:7 Peter emphasizes that God cares for you. You should turn all your worries over to him.

1 Peter 5:8 He cautions you to be on your guard and stay awake because the devil is sneaking around to find someone to attack.

Leader's Research and Student Notes.

_____

_____

_____

_____

_____

_____

_____

_____

_____

_____

_____

_____

_____

_____

_____

_____

_____

_____

_____

_____

_____

Beliefs, Thoughts, Drawings, Scribbles, Doodles.

LESSON 47: The Child

Pre-1500
1500 BC
1400 BC
1300 BC
1200 BC
1100 BC
1000 BC
900 BC
800 BC
700 BC
600 BC
500 BC
400 BC
300 BC
200 BC
100 BC
Christian Era
100 CE
200 CE
300 CE
400 CE
500 CE
600 CE
700 CE
800 CE
900 CE
1000 CE
1100 CE
1200 CE
1300 CE
1400 CE
1500 CE
1600 CE
1700 CE
1800 CE
1900 CE
2000 CE
2100 CE

Scripture: Revelation 12: 5-17

Suggested Key Verse: Revelation 12:11 [11] "Our people defeated Satan because of the blood of the lamb and the message of God. They were willing to give up their lives."

Suggested Key People: Michael and angels, the woman, the boy, our people, the devil (dragon, snake, Satan).

What does this story tell the youth of today? What walk through the Bible would be complete without discussing the Book of Revelation? This will take a lot of research prior to class followed by talk and discussion in class. This story does talk about a woman's son, assumed to be Jesus, and the struggle against evil. Do you believe in an actual devil that exists today? Is the snake that tempts Adam and Eve in the first book of the bible (Genesis 3) another picture of the devil? Is your life a struggle at times? Do you believe that evil will be defeated and you can win with God's help? Can you be faithful to the teachings of Jesus and accept his offer of salvation for you?

Lesson Summary:

Revelation 12:5-6 The woman gives birth to a son who will rule all nations. The boy is snatched away, taken to God, and placed on his throne. The woman runs to a place that God has prepared for her.

Revelation 12:7-9 A war in heaven leads to victory over the dragon (Satan, snake, devil) and its angels by Michael and his angels. The dragon and its angels are forced out of heaven and thrown down to earth.

Revelation 12:10-12 A voice from heaven announces our God's saving power and coming of his kingdom. "Our people" have given up their lives and defeated the devil because of the blood of the Lamb.

Revelation 12:13-14 The dragon realizes it has been thrown down to earth and tries to make trouble for the woman who gave birth to a son; she escapes into the desert to be taken care of.

Revelation 12:15-17 The dragon fails, gets angry, and starts a war against the rest of the woman's children, the people who obey God and are faithful to Jesus' teachings.

Leader's Research and Student Notes.

_____

_____

_____

_____

_____

_____

_____

_____

_____

_____

_____

_____

_____

_____

_____

Beliefs, Thoughts, Drawings, Scribbles, Doodles.

LESSON 48: God's Children

Pre-1500
1500 BC
1400 BC
1300 BC
1200 BC
1100 BC
1000 BC
900 BC
800 BC
700 BC
600 BC
500 BC
400 BC
300 BC
200 BC
100 BC
Christian Era
100 CE
200 CE
300 CE
400 CE
500 CE
600 CE
700 CE
800 CE
900 CE
1000 CE
1100 CE
1200 CE
1300 CE
1400 CE
1500 CE
1600 CE
1700 CE
1800 CE
1900 CE
2000 CE
2100 CE

Scripture: Galatians 4:1-7

Suggested Key Verse: Galatians 4:4-5 [4] But when the time was right, God sent his Son, and a woman gave birth to him. His Son obeyed the Law, [5] so he could set us free from the Law, and we could become God's children.

Suggested Key People: Paul talks about God's gift of Jesus.

What does this story tell the youth of today? Galatians was written by the Apostle Paul, possibly his first letter. Do you feel like a slave? No better off than a slave? Do you sometimes feel like you do not have enough control over what you can do, when you can do it, how you can do it? Do the "powers of the world" have a large impact on your life? Do your relationships with your friends have too large an impact on your life? God has provided the answers through the gift of his son, Jesus, and the Holy Spirit. He has given us family, friends, teachers, and others to help us live our lives free from sin and the powers of the world. God treats us as his children who will inherit everything.

Lesson Summary:

Galatians 4:1-2 Paul writes that children who are underage are no better off than being slaves even though they will inherit everything.

Galatians 4:3-5 But that is how it used to be. Paul tells that when the time was right, God sent his Son and a woman gave birth. His Son obeyed the Law so that he could set us free and we could become God's children.

Galatians 4:6-7 As God's children, he sent the spirit of the Son into our hearts telling us that God is our Father. We are no longer slaves but are God's children. We will be given what he promised.

Leader's Research and Student Notes.

_____

_____

_____

_____

_____

_____

_____

_____

_____

_____

_____

_____

_____

_____

_____

_____

_____

_____

_____

_____

_____

Beliefs, Thoughts, Drawings, Scribbles, Doodles.

Table 1: Stories Ordered by Timeline

Timeline	Lesson Order	Story	Bible References
BC 1500	1	Lot's Family	Genesis 19:12-29
BC 1500	2	Young Isaac	Genesis 18-22:18
BC 1500	3	Rebekah	Genesis 24
BC 1500	4	Jacob	Genesis 25:7-11,19-34 (Also see Genesis 32:22-32)
BC 1500	5	Joseph	Genesis 37:2b-34
BC 1400	6	Miriam	Exodus 2:1-10
BC 1400	7	Bezalel	Exodus 31:1-11 (Also see Exodus 35:30-36:1)
BC 1400	8	Servants to the Lord	Leviticus 27:1-7
BC 1400	9	Zelophehad's Daughters	Numbers 36:1-12
BC 1300	10	The Sin of Achan	Joshua 7
BC 1300	11	Achsah	Joshua 15:13-20
BC 1300	12	Jether and Jotham	Judges 8:13-20; 9:6-21
BC 1300	13	Jephthah's Daughter	Judges 11:29-40
BC 1300	14	Samson	Judges 13:1-24
BC 1100	15	Ruth	Ruth 1
BC 1100	16	Samuel	1 Samuel 1:6-22, 2:11, 3:1-10
BC 1000	17	David	1 Samuel 16:1-13
BC 1000	18	Temple Musicians	1 Chronicles 25:1-8 (Others thru Chapter 27)
BC 1000	19	Solomon	2 Samuel 12:13-25
BC 0900	20	Abishag	1 Kings 1-2
BC 0900	21	Abijah	1 Kings 14:1-18
BC 0900	22	Children/Young People	Proverbs 13:1-6, 20
BC 0800	23	Boys and the Bears	2 Kings 2
BC 0800	24	Elisha Brings Boy Back to Life	2 Kings 4:8-37 (See similar Elijah story at 1 Kings 17)
BC 0800	25	Naaman and the Servant Girl	2 Kings 5:1-15a
BC 0800	26	King Joash	2 Kings 11-12, 2 Chronicles 22-24
BC 0700 BC 0600		Note: There are other stories about young kings that could be included in your lessons if you so desire. For examples, see the following references for Uzziah, Manasseh, and Josiah. 2 Kings 22-23, 2 Chronicles 26, 2 Chronicles 32-36	
BC 0600	27	Jeremiah	Jeremiah 1; 18:1-10; 29:10-14; 33:14-16
BC 0600	28	Daniel	Daniel 1-2, 6 (Various verses)
BC 0600	29	Shadrach, Meshach, Abednego	Daniel 3
BC 0400	30	Esther	Esther 1-10 (Various verses)
CE	31	John the Baptist	Luke 1 (Various verses)

CE	32	Mary - Prophesies about Her Life	Luke 1:26-45; Luke 2:25-35
CE	33	Jesus in the Temple	Luke 2:41-52
CE	34	Jairus' Daughter	Luke 8:40-56
CE	35	Boy with a Demon	Luke 9:37-48
CE	36	The Prodigal Son	Luke 15:11-32
CE	37	Daughter of Herodias	Mark 6:14-29
CE	38	A Canaanite Woman's Faith	Matthew 15:21-28
CE	39	Ten Young Women	Matthew 25:1-13
CE	40	Boy with Fish and Bread	John 6:1-15
CE	41	Rhoda	Acts 12:11-17
CE	42	Slave Girl and Paul	Acts 16:16-22
CE	43	Eutychus	Acts 20
CE	44	Paul's Nephew	Acts 23:12-22
CE	45	Paul on the Island of Malta	Acts 28:1-11a
CE	46	Young People	1 Peter 5:5-8
CE	47	The Child	Revelation 12:5-17
CE	48	God's Children	Galatians 4:1-7 (See also Hebrews 12:4-11)

About the Author

As a children's teacher for thirty years in a church environment, Harold Williams developed a series of lessons about youth in the Bible from Genesis through Revelation. Success teaching in that first year encouraged him to expand, learn more stories, and formalize a leader's workbook for junior high and senior high students. He presents a different approach to teaching the Bible with the goal of learning about our Christian heritage as followers of Christ.

Printed in the United States
by Baker & Taylor Publisher Services